MORE RADIANT THAN THE SUN

MORE RADIANT THAN THE SUN

A Handbook
for Working with Steiner's
Meditations and Exercises

GERTRUDE REIF HUGHES

STEINERBOOKS | 2013

2013
SteinerBooks
An imprint of Anthroposophic Press, Inc.
610 Main St., Great Barrington, MA 01230
www.steinerbooks.org

Cover and book design: William Jens Jensen
Cover image © by Ciarada (shutterstock.com)

The following credit is gratefully acknowledged:

page 93. W.S. Merwin, "To the Gods" from *Present Company*.
Copyright © 2007 by W.S. Merwin.
Reprinted by permission of The Permissions Company, Inc.,
on behalf of Copper Canyon Press, www.coppercanyonpress.org.

ISBN 978-1-62148-035-8 (paperback)
ISBN 978-1-62148-036-5 (eBook)

Contents

Introduction

Anthroposophy: A Basis for Meditation

At this time in Western history, anyone can meditate. Rudolf Steiner frequently reminded audiences at his lectures and tirelessly described for his readers that in ancient times it was humans' spiritual surroundings, not their physical ones, that felt like home to them. Human souls were once embedded in the creativity of their spiritual origins, whereas ever since what is called "early modern" times (around the fifteen hundreds, the Shakespeare century, 1564 to 1616) those spiritual origins have been lost. Thanks to the evolution of consciousness in human souls and cultures, we now feel fully at home in the physical world but tend to neglect or even fail to notice that a spirit lives in us and we in it. Steiner worked against this failure. Though he always sincerely praised the extraordinary strides in the matter-based sciences, his own mission led him to enlarge the narrowness of materialistic visions of human life and planet Earth by clearly and patiently presenting the spiritual existence of cosmic grandeur and esoteric mysteries that modern minds should take seriously, reverently, and scientifically.

Steiner's famous opening paragraph of the weekly letters* he sent when he was ill and no longer able to lecture shows his certainty that human beings carry a full meditative life in their being but are only rarely conscious of it. His mission, of course, was to recognize and support the truths that filled many human souls in his time, but—and he knew this well—various strong counterforces clouded the goodwill, freedom, and fellowship of

---

* Steiner, *Anthroposophical Leading Thoughts* (hereafter cited as *Leading Thoughts*).

human hearts, along with a lack of reverence and a fear of interest in the invisible based on wishful thinking instead of reality. In Steiner's time and in ours, the work of spiritual perception and meditation in human souls and in their conversation with others is expected to come first from the humans living on planet Earth. Humanity needs more human beings who will consciously develop a capacity to cognize the current scope and nature of spirit existence, that of the gods and ours. On our own and in groups, human beings are finding their ways to a spirituality that, in fact, already exists as part of their physical, mental, and spiritual constitutions in these times. We find a creative mental life in our souls and with it a morality not of right and wrong, not even of good and evil, but of a free consciousness ready to explore morality and experiment with its essences by means of our awakened powers, both individual and social. Steiner's Anthroposophy offers deep and lively universal wisdom to support individuals who seek to explore and experience spirituality and to connect themselves consciously to universal mysteries. His Anthroposophy is a basis for modern meditation wherever and whenever it is happening.

All over the world, people are meditating. Many use their meditation as a chance to relax, have a quiet time, or take a moment to give thanks for gifts in their lives and the lives of their family and friends. While these resorts qualify as a search for peace, which may even become prayer-like, the meditation in which this handbook has particular interest faces toward transformations that begin with the meditator's seeking self-training that turns the self toward spirit willing and spirit knowing, aroused and guided by Steiner's Anthroposophy, wherever it is found. Ultimately, this self-training cultivates a spirit feeling, one that prepares to give the way love gives, and builds strength—be it of patience, generosity, or courage.

The training, we could say, comes inward to go outward. Framing meditation in these anthroposophic ways has a background in ancient mysteries, which a meditating person today has probably already engaged with in a former lifetime and wants to transform in this life. Their interests and goals have to do with helping their fellow humans' needs for recognition, healing, deepening, educating, and feeling or making themselves ready for the new.

Those human beings now living on Earth who do not feel a need for spirituality insist that they must stop short at a borderline where matter ends and spirit begins on the other side. Having come to a gap and seeing no effective way that will take them further, they settle for either matter or spirit, but not both. Their impoverished souls cling to a bias (not to say fear) that insists on disconnecting spirit from knowledge or science. To them, Steiner's term *Spiritual Science* sounds like an oxymoron at best, whereas those who perceive the borderline or gap as a frontier accept it as inviting their further and spiritual participation. Far from stopping short at the border, they regard it as a door, enter it with open souls, and find nurturance by meditating the truths to be found on the other side—indeed on both sides.

Working by means of our souls, with verses and exercises from Steiner like the ones you will find in part two of this handbook, trains us "to guide the Spiritual in the human being to the Spiritual in the universe." We, not the gods, are the ones who must start. Steiner famously describes such training in the first sentence of his *Leading Thoughts*.* For some, the training feels strange and uncertain. Others instantly recognize their desire for it. Either way, Steiner's *Leading Thoughts* speaks of his Anthroposophy as a guide that already inhabits the human being. Anthroposophy arises there "as a need of the heart, of the life of feeling and...can be justified only inasmuch as it can satisfy this inner need [with] certain questions on the nature of the human being and the universe"—questions that humanity experiences

---

* Ibid., p. 13, #1.

as "an elemental need of life, just as one feels hunger and thirst."*
Clearly, Steiner's characterization of Anthroposophy shows it is
both needed and loved by those who are reaching out for it and
even by those who want it unconsciously. In their inner, microcosmic souls, human beings harbor spirit. From there they reach
toward the spirit in the outer, macrocosmic universe by means of
their meditative efforts.

Although the term *Spiritual Science* may sound paradoxical
or whimsical to some, Steiner himself did not share such views.
He carried his Anthroposophy wherever he went, supported by
the clairvoyance of his inner life and his outer life's talent for
goodwill and his pleasure in company with people of various
paths and levels of life. The clairvoyance he experienced from
his young days remained with him throughout his life. Though
he eventually accustomed himself to the more materialistic views
that most people automatically assume in themselves and others,
Steiner's lifelong, intimate capacity for spiritual perception and
his true confidence in Anthroposophy understands the seeming
barrier between the material and spiritual worlds, which can be
perceived as a doorway by which Anthroposophy must "live on
both sides" or "it cannot really live at all."**

As an extremely spiritually fit person living firmly on Earth,
Steiner created his own spiritual life and brought it to Earth as
"Anthroposophy," because the Greek *sophia* (Σοφία) refers to the
wisdom residing in humanity and a fundamental and ever-devel-
oping essence of *being* human makes us *anthropoi*.

In the second famous paragraph Steiner acknowledges how
everyday life trusts the science founded on sensation and intellectual activity rather, he implies, than on spiritually aware science,
like what Anthroposophy offers. Yet, even as he acknowledges
the difficulty of the barrier that makes some feel they must stop
short at it, he is aware of those others who see that same barrier

---

*   Ibid.
**   Ibid., p. 13, #2.

as a frontier. For them, "at the very frontier where the knowledge derived from sense-perception ceases, there is opened through the human soul itself the further outlook into the spiritual world." Yes. The "human soul itself" has achieved this status. Unlike those who are stopped by their scientism at the barrier, the human souls who go on have ability to look into spirit realities. Steiner clearly wants his readers to notice that the achievement is theirs:

> Anthroposophy communicates knowledge that is gained in a spiritual way. Yet it does so only because everyday life and the science founded on sensation and intellectual activity lead to a barrier along life's way—a limit where the life of the soul in the human being would die if it could go no further. Everyday life and science do not lead to this limit in such a way as to compel the human being to stop short at it. For at the very frontier where the knowledge derived from sensory perception ceases, the further outlook into the spiritual world is opened through the human soul itself.*

Therefore, our spirituality lives in our soul, as does the world's spirit, but those who do not feel the need to gain what Anthroposophy offers will insist that a boundary in their daily life must stop them short. Accordingly, those souls hear a term such as *Spiritual Science* as a meaningless oxymoron at best, whereas those for whom the border is a frontier recognize that it invites their further participation. Far from limiting themselves at the border, they occupy the frontier with open souls and nurture themselves with truths that they themselves are discovering.

Each verse or exercise in part two of this handbook offers a particular form for meditating with your soul. Hold a small seed in your hand and look at it carefully, reflecting on the fact that both Sun and Earth bring the seed's growth. Sink into an aphorism such as "In thinking I feel myself united with the

---

*   Ibid., p. 13, #2.

stream of cosmic existence." Read Steiner's carefully narrated picture of the red rose on the black cross and make sure you follow each stage with your inner feeling. Usually, one needs to focus on a verse or other theme to engage it. Once you do that, you are working with the theme of the verse; you are meditating it. The focus you muster opens your soul to experiencing itself at work with the theme and what it brings to you. You encounter your soul and the spirit that lives in it along with your will, which abides there as an active vitality, the source of which is unconscious in you. Although your will is unconscious, it enables contemplative activity in your soul to encounter and engage with the verse you have chosen. Eventually, you find that you can call your meditating a practice. When we earthlings take on the task of meditating, other spiritual beings take it on, too. They join us! We are not alone. Our individual souls collaborate with cosmic spirits.

In a lecture from 1922, Steiner describes how human relationships to spiritual existence have been evolving since the late years of the nineteenth century. He pictures the evolved spiritual existence with words about connecting, entering, and ability, rather than about viewing or worshiping. Clearly, the scene has changed since the late nineteenth century, because "human beings are now newly able to receive the spiritual world if they so desire," and what is more they have a new task:

> Spirit is present in all material manifestations of our life, which cannot persist without our participation in the spirit. Today we must understand that this spirit does not merely attempt to address the cosmos out of human longing. *It attempts to flow into our earthly world from a different world.* We must understand that the windows between our world and this other world have been opened, not by us alone but also by the spiritual world that surrounds us.... When we consider the history of our times, we must realize that human beings are now *newly able to*

receive the spiritual world if they so desire. Consequently, cultivating the *spirit on Earth* is now a superearthly task, an intrinsic part of the life of the spiritual world itself.*

Connecting where once there had been a gap will happen *through* us as well as *to* us. We can recognize that the cosmos interests itself in how we live here on Earth. Spirit manifests in earthly existence, so it surrounds us as part of our environment, and we can take its collaborating seriously. Indeed, spirit beings in realms of spirit expect us human beings to receive them, to interest ourselves in them, and to have them collaborate with us in our earthly lives.

The question arises, how might we as incarnated, earthly humans integrate our spirituality, including our meditations, with the rest of our life? Thanks to Steiner's generous sharing of the suprasensory vision from which he gave his lectures, he was able to turn his living knowledge into thoughts that his audiences can follow today, just as they could when he first uttered them. If we approach our contemplative soul inquiries and experiences about the spiritual world in humility and reverence as best we can, then integrating our souls' meditations into our lives by means of Anthroposophy itself confirms that our souls and world cultures can create forms uniting Heaven and Earth. In short, the spiritual practices of human beings become agents of heavenly spirit on Earth.

In various settings where meditation is being practiced or learned, I am sometimes asked to identify what the words *spirit* and *spirituality* mean to me. For me, spirit is the divine in the human. What I think of as spirit is our inner relationship to that divinity; it lives—acknowledged or not—in every human being. Spirituality and individuality belong together. When I meditate, I feel the divinity in my veritable constitution, reachable there

---

*   Steiner, *The Sun Mystery and the Mystery of Death and Resurrection,* "Anthroposophy as an Attempt to Enchristen the World," Vienna, July 11, 1922, pp. 140–141 (emphasis added).

because created there by a divine creator, who placed its divinity in me, as in all its creatures. Spirit belongs to the karma of my life, as it does for all people. Of course, all personal situations experience evils and hardships that come with earthly life, some of them brought on by the activities of evil tempters, who offer illusions and whose brilliant, intelligent lies can impress and organize both inner and outer human lives. Still, tested with bliss and trapped in untruth, our very experiences with having been caught and dazed by lies and illusions ultimately bring strength to us, not weakness. True, once we are born, our shining, pre-birth, spiritually crafted decisions become darkened, twisted, or even poisonous, placing us in heavy, burdensome confinements. Nevertheless, thanks to the "mystical fact" of the "Mystery of Golgotha," we are potentially always protected and renewed. All human beings in any earthly situation can count on help and transformation from the "Representative of Humanity," as Steiner calls the Christ being. His transforming presence can save every willing human despite all the misdeeds. My life has shown me this presence, and when it has not done so, even the potential of its presence has been real to me.

Human souls exist between Heaven and Earth. The efforts and explorations we make when we meditate orient us to the suprasensory. There our contemplative practicing tells us, experientially, that the earthly and the heavenly can meet in harmony. By harmonizing those two sides of our lives, we human beings create a meeting of the heavenly and the earthly in our souls. In this way, thanks to transformations within ourselves and in the planet itself, Anthroposophy envisions that Earth will eventually become a home for us, where our meditative cognizing opens a direct, soul-spiritual capacity for objective—not just subjective—experiences and experiments with our planet Earth's own heavenly realities.

Steiner discovers that, during our lifetime between birth and death, our three-part constitution of body, soul, and spirit make contemplative acts possible. An independent element in our makeup, the will, prevents dying in our physical body, while our soul-spiritual self, too, has a special feature—a living, essential thinking with which spirit has endowed intuitive power. Both of these discoveries—one physical, one not—show that they want to support our earthly meditating. Therefore, when we meditate this is what happens: We rise out of our body, but it continues to live. The independent element in the human constitution is called the etheric, or life, body (or sometimes the body of formative forces), and it is "accessible to higher vision but recognizable to sensory perception only because of its effects."*

The etheric body brings growth and other living possibilities to the physical body, yet the etheric "body" itself is actually not at all bodily. Rather, Steiner says that suprasensory knowledge "attributes a higher degree of reality to it than to the physical body."** Much is at stake in Steiner's view that the etheric forms the physical. He continues as follows:

> For the moment let it suffice to say that the ether body permeates the physical body in all its parts and is to be seen as its architect, so to speak. The shape and form of all our organs are maintained by the ether body's currents and movements. Our physical heart is based on an "ether heart," our physical brain, on an "ether brain," and so on.... In the ether body everything is in a living, flowing state of interpenetration, whereas in the physical body, distinctly separate parts are present.***

The etheric *belongs* to the suprasensory though it *functions* in the physical. (Incidentally, that very sentence could well be explored meditatively.) That placing of suprasensory capacity—in us humans, and when we are living on earth—creates a new

---

*   Steiner, *An Outline of Esoteric Science*, p. 33 (cited hereinafter as *Esoteric Science*).
**   Ibid., p. 35.
*** Ibid., pp. 35–36.

consciousness in humans: We can bring spirit into the physical. As a spiritual organization, the etheric connects the physical to spiritual realities, which include the growth and formative forces that work from within the physical. In a similar way, and with similar results, the intuitive nature of thinking mentioned above also belongs to our human constitution. Such essential thinking is ready to be active, and consciously so. Steiner describes essential, intuitive thinking as follows:

> There is an inner entity inherent in thought itself that already has connections to the suprasensory world. The soul is usually not aware of these connections because it is in the habit of developing its thinking abilities only by applying them to the sensory world. As a result, the soul finds information about the suprasensory world incomprehensible. However, this information actually is understandable not only to a spiritually trained way of thinking, but to any thinking that is aware of its full power and is willing to make use of it.*

Too often, Steiner's "knowledge" is mistaken for a mass of static truth waiting to be claimed. Whatever knowledge Anthroposophy intends to awaken in us, its existence sleeps in us until *we* interest ourselves in it and begin to feel its promise. What Steiner calls "living thinking," or sometimes "essential thinking," belongs to that awakening.

Halfway through my twenties, when I first began to meditate, I found concentrating a difficult but interesting and even dramatic practice. Steiner's various directions for concentrating on an ordinary, human-made object as a theme offer three steps that can organize what one might do with one's attention. First, what does this cup, table, paper clip, or pencil look like? Second, how was it made or how might I myself make it. Surprisingly, you experience the act of concentrating as quite worthy of your time when you

---

*   Ibid., p. 321.

involve yourself in such questions with real interest. You have a third angle from which to work when you then add, "What is the function of this human-made thing?"—that is, the pencil, paper clip, and so on. What does it *do* in earthly human life? What did its inventor perceive that led her or him to create that spoon, comb, or cup—and not just this one, but all spoons, combs, or cups.

Adding the question about an object's function makes meditating human-made objects more cosmic than you might think, because the not-yet-made object, which gave its inventor the idea of making it, plays a part in your meditation.* Dwelling on the function of a fork, a pipe, or a table opens the possibility to acknowledge a pre-physical background from which an object came into its present, physical existence. Concentrating on an item's function enriches what your attention on the object as an idea can experience. The function of a spoon brings to your observing and thinking how such objects do their work. Realizing a human-made object's function enlarges your meditating with a connected set of qualities to be cognized and experienced. (Of course, the function of the object might also make you wander away from the item, in which case it would be a reason to save the function part for a time when your practicing has a still stronger focusing capacity.)

---

* According to Georg Kühlewind: "We can make the idea, the function of the object, into the theme of the concentration exercise. [At first] it doesn't work at all, and we ... imagine a particular functioning object (a spoon for ladling soup) or we try to come up with a thought-out formulation of the function. Neither of these is the idea.... Ease the transition to the idea by imagining a whole row of functioning objects (small, big, ladles, etc.) and then try to see the common element in them—the idea. This requires pure thinking because the idea, the function, is not an image or a word.... That which is in consciousness can be an inner experience of light, or an experience of shadows in light, or a color, a smell and so on. Generally, this is preceded by the experience of finding that one becomes the object or the function oneself" (*From Normal to Healthy*, pp. 167–168).

As students training for spiritual work, we are free and ready to use our normally suprasensory powers, the etheric in our physical body and the intuitive in our thinking. Interest supplies the soul with what it needs for building such capacity by meditating in a committed way. In that sense meditation is the core of Anthroposophy, just as Anthroposophy is a basis for meditation. Yet, even those who earnestly study spirit science and feel its cultural potential do not readily find meditating the core activity to engage in. They fail to realize that what Steiner calls the path of knowledge simply involves beginning! Start is the point (or *Start Now!* as Christopher Bamford titles his collection of many verses, exercises, and training methods); Anthroposophy calls you, as a free individual, to take yourself in hand and make a plan that you intend to uphold. Such plans consider how you will reserve a period, perhaps a full half hour each day (or certain specific days each week) when you can give yourself a chance to calm your soul, find reverence and humility in it, and—into that peaceful inner silence—place a theme upon which you will focus your mind and soul. To create such a plan makes a good beginning. A detailed plan does make a realistic step forward, but it does not have to be made as a promise.

Any meditating practice begins with concentration. Focus on a sentence—yours or one you find in a wise book, in Steiner's works, or in the Bible. Make the theme an idea, an ideal, or a feeling—grief, joy, hope. Concentrating usually turns out to be a more energetic effort than we had expected. To stay with the theme has to be practiced again and again before we become somewhat skilled at controlling our attention.* Three minutes focusing on, say, a simple and not particularly interesting,

---

*   Note that "The Six Essential Exercises," which you will find among the collected verses in part two of this book, devotes exercise number one to concentrating on an object and sustaining your focus on it as long as you can.

human-made object turns out to require hard work. Unless you have experience with self-controlled concentration your mind usually wanders; you may find that it has wandered far away by the time three minutes are up. At that point, you discover an important fact: *I am my attention. Where my attention is, there am I.*

You can test the truth of this assertion by performing a little thought exercise: You are walking with a friend, immersed in conversation, and listening intently when suddenly your attention loses the theme. Though your friend continues her story and you continue walking along, your attention has turned to planning tonight's dinner, which reminds you that you still haven't found the right gift for tomorrow's birthday party, which brings you to the funeral in the community, which sets you musing on the mystery that death is part of life, when—who knows why—your focus returns to listening. To repeat: *Where my attention is, there am I. Essentially, I am my attention.*

"I am my attention" means that training the attention involves training *you,* and that "you" is your "I," your self. Sitting more or less comfortably, practicing after a meal or before one, choosing themes that you really care about—you discover that none of these sensible adjustments gives you control over your attention, because your attention comes from within your soul, not from an outer condition. The content of your meditation has no power over exercising your attention. You yourself have this power, because you *are* your attention. The wandering of your attention shows that your attention and the theme of your meditation have not stayed together but, of course, they could have. Your attention is the potential I of your true individuality and it can learn to follow its own intentions.

The human I lives in each person as the unique feature of which every single human being has its own version. Consider a two-level thought exercise based on this fact. First, ask yourself, *What is it I am doing when I feel most myself?* Your answer might be skiing, building a stone wall, gardening, singing, listening to opera, or talking with your spouse on the phone. I hear all these answers and others like them when I teach a meditation course or lead a workshop. The answers lead to a deeper question: What does it feel like when I feel most myself? "Feeling my self" has a certain quality for each human being. I have asked dozens of meditation students that second question and others, too. When people go on to describe not the activities that allow them to feel themselves, but the words that might describe the actual feeling they experience, the words tend surprisingly to be similar for the whole group. No matter what activity brings out this feeling, it seems "pleasurable," "peaceful," "calm," "engaged," and "absorbed" for all. Never do such words occur as *anxious, nervous, frightened, unsure,* or *tense*—let alone the words *angry, upset, trapped,* or *suspicious.* Like the idea "I am my attention," the experience that "I am least aware of myself when I feel most myself" has within it what we need for meditation—the seed of the "I," a selfless selfhood.

Let us consider a third situation, in which the presence or absence of the attention or one's "I" plays a part: You have focused on an object or sentence and you have strongly entered the details and meanings that you found. Gradually, the vitality of the meditation dwindles and you end it. When you do so, you suddenly realize that you are hearing traffic out on the street, the furnace working down in the cellar, or the voices of children playing on the porch. As you take in all those sounds from your outer life, you realize that they were there all along, but your attention had not been. Your attention had been active in your inner life, experiencing in your soul the verse and its meanings. By directing your attention toward the theme of the meditation and staying with it, sensory participation in your surroundings had actually been blocked, because your soul work had opened toward the suprasensory instead. These three thought exercises show in different ways how meditation and the "I" belong together.

To meditate spiritually requires focus initially, but when you realize this and act accordingly you find that this spiritual capacity you have—your attention—can also turn its focus into something seemingly opposite. Once your focus is strong, it can become a receptive vessel made of opened attention that can expect to wait. A wise friend and mentor used to say to me in numerous life situations, "I wait to know." Those four monosyllables apply to waiting with concentrated but empty attention until there is something to know and you are able to notice its arrival or presence.

The stronger your focused attention has been, the more likely will your open attention be able to notice the subtle presence that will perhaps arrive and perhaps engage your soul. To summarize: What happens when we meditate? We concentrate, then we open, and then we engage our soul's thinking, willing, and feeling with what comes next. All these approaches and additions to meditating an object bring you to erasing your own meditated experiences so as to replace them and look further.

At first, the soul-spirit sensing available to our meditating souls' potentials may be weak, confusing, or just unnoticed. However, as we practice exercises and meditative verses such as those from Steiner in part two of this handbook, we begin to take possession of our freedom. We secure our identity as meditators and develop our confidence as human beings in a full world of spiritual-physical activity. This confidence is not so much psychological as it is, for lack of a better word, primary. It has to do with standing on your own feet in a universe much bigger than we are and knowing that our sensing soul can move images out of the way to reveal how our attention can inspire us to further concepts and participations. Alive, working, and awake, the incarnate soul can live outside of its body, thanks to the soul's divinely given meditative capacities. That is what we do when we meditate and why this handbook's introductory pages speak of basic facts about the meditating body, soul, and spirit.

For two of the exercises included in part two of this book (the Rose Cross symbol and the growth and decay meditation), Steiner suggested adding the technique of "erasing" what your meditation imagination has pictured and replacing it with a fresh approach that deepens the whole through the vitality that comes with inspiration. Certainly, soul sensations that come directly from first focusing the attention and then opening it to receive ideas and images with willed, intentional thinking on the theme can bring a rich tapestry of related yet freshly realized ideas and insights. All this, however, can be erased and another view put in its place. For example, at the end of his classic presentation of the Rose Cross, Steiner recommends trying to eliminate the black cross and red roses from your consciousness, erasing the sensations you have found in the symbol and then lingering meditatively, trying to notice what your soul actually did to create and integrate the symbol of black cross and red rose. He elaborates that such a shift of the meditation will gradually lead to inspiration, moving from a focusing soul toward an integrating one:

> Within our souls, we should ask: What have I done inwardly in order to combine the cross and roses into this symbol? I want to hold fast to what I have done, to the personal soul process I have undergone, but to allow the image itself to disappear from my consciousness. I will feel everything within me that my soul did in order to bring the image about, but I will not picture the image itself. From this point onward, I will dwell quite inwardly in the activity of mine that created the image. Instead of meditating on an image, I will become absorbed in my own image-creating soul activity.[*]

Similarly, Steiner advises dwelling on our own spiritual activity when we work with "Perceiving Growth and Decay." We start by imagining a plant emerging from a seed and flourishing, and

---

[*]   Steiner, *Esoteric Science*, p. 340.

then we see it wilting as it proceeds toward dissolution. Those two transformations gradually bring our imagination to a feeling that the plant's becoming and decaying are images of transformation processes that underlie the images being viewed. At this point, Steiner proposes a move from imagination to inspiration:

> If we want to achieve the corresponding inspiration we must do the exercise differently. We must reflect on the actual soul activity that derived the idea of becoming and decay from the image of the plant. We must *allow the plant to disappear completely from our consciousness and meditate only on our own inner activity.* Only exercises of this sort make it possible to rise to the level of inspiration.*

In both these meditations, where inspiration displaces imagination the changes entail attending to inner meditative activity. Erasing the sight of the flourishing and decay or deciding to stop viewing the rose cross opens a different level whereby the soul can experience and evaluate bold, though subtle, shifts in the meditating soul. Those shifts are beginnings of contemplative research and inquiry.

As for intuition, the deepest power of a thinking that can be developed, its depth and applications live at various levels in humanity's being. In the following, Steiner connects intuition with microcosmic and macrocosmic life, underlining the capacity both to correspond and to remain distinct:

> At the appropriate level of inner development, students of the spirit begin to recognize relationship between their own individual beings and the greater world. This level of cognition can be described as becoming aware of the correspondence between the microcosm, the smaller world of the human being, and the macrocosm, or cosmic infinity. Having broken through to this stage of

* Ibid., p. 341 (emphasis added).

knowledge, students of the spirit can then begin to have a new experience. In spite of being aware of themselves in their full independence, *they begin to feel as if they have grown together with the entire structure of the cosmos.* They have a feeling of merging with the entire cosmos and becoming one with it, yet *without losing their essential nature.*

Poets are able to experience and express this "feeling of merging with the...cosmos." In his "Song of My Self" (1855) Walt Whitman (1819–1892) utters his micro–macro experience in an image of large brightness—so large as to be dangerous:

> Dazzling and tremendous
>   how quick the sun-rise would kill me,
> If I could not now and always
>   send sun-rise out of me.**

Emily Dickinson (1830–1886) also considered avoiding danger by choosing her own way to inhabit possibility so as to be available, as it were, to find or be found by poems rather than allowing herself to be sheltered by prose:

> I dwell in Possibility—
> A fairer House than Prose—
> More numerous for Windows—
> Superior—for Doors—
>
> Of Chambers as the Cedars—
> Impregnable of Eye—
> And for an Everlasting Roof—
> The Gambrels of the Sky—

---

*   Ibid., p. 372 (emphasis added).

**   Whitman, "Song of Myself," *Leaves of Grass*, "chant," or section, 25, p. 45. In one of his essays collected in *The Necessary Angel*, Wallace Stevens (1899–1955) calls the mind of poets "a violence from within that protects us from a violence without." As far as I know, Stevens is not echoing Whitman intentionally.

Of Visitors—the fairest—
For Occupation—This—
The spreading wide my narrow Hands
To gather Paradise—*

Delicate but at the same time completely certain, she knows
that possibility is "a fairer House than Prose," because that fairer
house has walls, the landscape has impregnable cedars, and the
sky serves well—indeed "Everlasting"—for a roof. In case a
reader needs to know her size, she warns or concedes that she
spreads wide her narrow hands, thereby assuring her readers and
herself that she knows what she means by "To gather Paradise"—
namely, to manage well, even if she has to die in the act. In her
case, death and the everlasting are not as separate in their size as
some might think. Her dozens of poems about death show this in
many brilliant ways. Poems are portals to meditations, and poets
tend to know this, but that is another story.

The main points for these introductory pages have been made:
the human soul meditates. The hierarchies are interested in this
situation and collaborate with it through us. Anthroposophy
supports it all, but those individuals whose souls meditate have,
like Whitman and Dickinson, a clear understanding that their
"I" is at work.

Perhaps it will be worthwhile to end this introduction on a
cautionary note about wishful thinking in our meditation praxis;
it may not have been emphasized enough. Speaking of the lotus
flower as the soul-spiritual organ that takes shape when the soul
or the astral body starts to sense its activity in our inner life,
Steiner warns,

> We must not imagine such an organ as something whose
> reality is reflected by our sensory mental image of it. These
> "organs" are supersensible and consist of soul activity that
> is shaped in a particular way. They exist only inasmuch

---

* *The Complete Poems of Emily Dickinson,* # 657, p. 327.

and as long as this soul activity is being exercised. There is nothing sense-perceptible about these organs, just as no "vapor" is present around a human being who is thinking. We fall into misunderstandings if we insist on imagining the supersensible as sense-perceptible in any way.[*]

He does grant that, as long as our hopes do not blur what our meditative experiences bring to us, we may well "receive repeated 'flashes of light' from a higher world. Even such 'flashes' allow...[students] to bear witness to spiritual worlds and should be accepted with gratitude."[**] (ibid.). The point is not to have "a preconceived idea of what we are actually trying to 'see'" but to wait patiently because "it often takes a long, long time before these organs have developed enough to be used for perception in the higher world."[***] The difficulty, of course, is not just wishful thinking, but also what Emily Dickinson means when she says,

> Not "Revelation"—'tis—that waits,
> But our unfurnished eyes—[****]

Her cautionary sentence has no trouble believing the "revelation" that some can see. Rather, she puts the problem on those who are trying to "see." Have we "furnished our eyes" sufficiently and appropriately, or do we let wishful thinking come between our hopes and the actual situation in which we are entertaining a revelation whose existence is before us but perhaps not in the forms we expect. It makes sense for Dickinson to have the last word for now. In part three of this book, we will return to matters of meditation.

---

[*]   Steiner, *Esoteric Science*, p. 326.

[**]   Ibid., p. 327.

[***]   Ibid.

[****] *The Complete Poems of Emily Dickenson*, #685, p. 339.

Three Meditations on Self

More Radiant than the Sun

Working with an Esoteric Lesson,
Berlin, October 24, 1905

GRH: Here is the verse itself, in what is thought to be Steiner's own translation from the German. It is accompanied on this page with a brief report on how I worked with it before I knew that a summary existed of an esoteric class in which Steiner explained how the verse could be perceived.

I used this verse as a meditation long before Steiner's summary of an exemplary esoteric lesson about meditating this verse became available in print. Omitting the last four lines at first, I treated the first three lines as a koan—a Zen-like riddle fashioned in the form of a paradox. I would ask myself, *What really is more radiant than the sun? How, when, where?* In that way, working as deeply and sincerely as I could with those first three lines, I would bring myself closer to a realm of imagination, essence, or source. Then when I allowed myself to enter the lines about the self, I could feel that my previous effort might plausibly count as "the Spirit of my Heart." From there I could more or less experience the Self as a "mystical fact," in which one's own identity participates. Of course, the problem was this: by treating the first lines as a koan would I ever have thought of my own selfhood in connection with those lines if I hadn't at least once seen the fourth through seventh lines.

Read the Esoteric Lesson below to see Steiner's explanation of the verse. According to a note in the third edition of "Guidance in Esoteric Training: From the Esoteric School," Steiner's explanation of how to meditate on this verse constitutes "the only summary of the content of an Esoteric Class written by Rudolf Steiner himself."

More radiant than the Sun,
Purer than snow,
Finer than ether
Is the self
The spirit of my heart.
I am this self,
This self am I.

***

Rudolf Steiner's Esoteric Lesson
on the Verse's Content

Berlin, October 24, 1905

We see the objects that surround us only when they are shone upon by the sun. What makes them visible are the Sun's rays reflected back from the objects into the eye of the beholder. If there were no light the objects would not be visible. For us to see things of a soul and spiritual nature, a light "more radiant than the Sun" must shine upon us. This light does not proceed from any external sun. It comes from the source of light that we kindle in ourselves when we seek within for our higher eternal self. This higher self has a different origin than our lower self. The latter experiences our everyday surroundings. However, everything that lives in this everyday environment has at some time come into being and will one day pass away.... Thus our experience of it has only a transitory value. And from such transitory experiences and our thoughts about them our transitory self is built up. All things that become visible because of the sun were, at one time, not in existence, and some day they will pass away. Even the Sun came into existence at a certain time and will one day also pass away. But the soul exists for the very purpose of recognizing the eternal in things. When one day the entire Earth will be no more, the souls who inhabited it will still exist. And what these souls have experienced on earth they will carry with them elsewhere as a memory.

It is the same as when a person does a good deed for me. The deed passes away, but what he or she has planted in my soul remains. And the bond of love that has thus united us does not pass away. What we experience is always the source of something that endures within us. We ourselves extract that which endures from things and carry that over into eternity. And when one day human beings are transplanted to a quite different arena of action, they will bring with them what they have gathered here. And their deeds in the new world will be woven out of the memories of the old. For there is no seed that does not bear fruit.

If we are united with someone by love, then this love is a seed and we will experience the fruit all through the future because we belong together with such a person throughout the future. Thus, something lives in us that is interwoven with the divine power. That binds all things together into the eternal fabric of the universe. This "something" is our higher self. And *this* is more radiant than the Sun. The light of the Sun illuminates from the outside only. The sun of the soul illuminates from within. Therefore it is more radiant than the Sun.

Purer than snow

In itself everything is pure. It can become impure only when it unites with something that should not be united with it. In and of itself water is pure. But even the dirt in dirty water would be pure if it were in and of itself, if it had not united with the water in an unlawful way. Carbon by itself is pure. It becomes dirt only if it is wrongfully united with water. Now, when water assumes its own form in a snow crystal, it separates out all that has united wrongly with it. So too does the human soul become pure if it separates out all that is improperly united with it. And the divine, the imperishable belongs to the soul. Every ideal, every thought of something great and beautiful belongs to the inner form of the soul. And when it meditates upon such ideals, such thoughts, then it purifies itself as the water purifies itself in becoming a snow crystal. And because the spiritual is purer than anything material, the "higher self"—that is, the soul that lives in the heights—is "purer than snow."

Finer [subtler] than the ether

Ether is the finest [subtlest] form of matter. But all matter is still dense compared to the element of soul. It is not the "dense" that is lasting but the "fine." The stone that we think of as matter will pass away as matter. But the *thought* of the stone, which lives in the soul, remains. God has thought this thought. And out of it he made the dense stone. Just as ice is only water made dense, so the stone is only a thought of God's made dense. All objects are such thickened thoughts of God. The "higher self," however, dissolves all things, and the thoughts of God then live in that higher self. And when the self is woven out of such thoughts of God, then it is "finer than the ether."

The spirit in my heart

We have really understood something only when we have grasped it with our heart. Intellect and reason are merely mediators for the heart's understanding. Through intellect and reason we penetrate to divine thoughts. But once we have really taken hold of the thought, then we must learn to *love* it. Gradually we learn to love all things. This does not mean that we should give our heart without discrimination to everything we encounter. For our experience is deceptive at first. However, when we make an effort to understand a being or a thing down to its origin in the divine, then we also begin to love it. If I have a depraved human being standing in front of me, then in no way should I love his or her depravity. Through such an act I would only be in error and would not help the person at all. However, if I reflect on how this person has come to his or her depravity and if I help him or her to leave it behind, then I am helping the person and I myself struggle through to the truth.

I must seek everywhere to find *how* I can love. God is present in all things, but this divinity in any particular thing I must first seek. It is not the external aspect of a being or thing that I should love straightaway, for this can be deceptive and I could easily love the error. However, truth lies *behind* all illusion, and we can always love truth. If the heart seeks the love of truth in all beings, then there lives the "spirit in the heart." Such love is the garment the soul should always wear. Then the soul itself weaves the divine into things.

❧

The members of the school should take several minutes a day to connect such thoughts to the divine maxims of wisdom, which have been given to us by the masters out of their boundless world-experience. Members should never think that they have completely understood a maxim but always assume that still more lies in it than they have already found. Through an attitude such as this we come to feel that in all genuine wisdom is the key to the infinite, and in this feeling we bind ourselves to the infinite.

It is not a matter of meditating on many sentences, but of letting a little live again and again in a soul that has become still.

During the meditation itself one should speculate very little, but instead quietly allow the content of the sentences to work upon one. But apart from the meditation, during free moments in the course of the day one should return to the content of the sentences and see what reflections one can draw from them. Then they become a living power that imbues the soul and makes it strong and vigorous. For when the soul unites with eternal truth, it lives in the eternal. And when the soul lives in the eternal, then higher beings have access to it and can let their own power permeate it.[*]

---

[*] Steiner, *Esoteric Lessons, 1904–1909*, pp. 34–37.

2

Life Becomes

GRH: For me, meditation has been an adventure from the start. I opened myself to the path of knowledge, having no capacity, I thought, for spiritual perception already developed in me. However, I had read some basic Anthroposophy, especially *The Philosophy of Freedom*,* and throughout my twenty-eight or twenty–nine years, my mother and I had been talking Anthroposophy, so I had experience and deep interest in it. Just creating a space of privacy—never mind peace or contemplation—was hard to do, but making that possible was exactly what I felt the need to do.

My husband and I lived in a small house with small children in an era before fathers were expected to share responsibility for childcare and housework. At this point we were the parents of one kindergartner, one nursery school child, one crawler-toddler, and a new baby on the way. Though most of my life was committed to parenting and household tasks, I yearned for childfree moments if not a childfree life. I was still reading Anthroposophy, now in the form of the New York City Rudolf Steiner School's bulletin, *Education as an Art*, which my mother kindly sent to me, and A. C. Harwood's *Recovery of Man in Childhood: A Study in the Educational Work of Rudolf Steiner* (1958). One day, my mother sent me the following meditation, written by hand so that each line made one side of a triangle:

---

*   Current translation, *Intuitive Thinking as a Spiritual Path: A Philosophy of Freedom.*

> Life becomes clearer around me
> *(right leg of triangle)*
> Life becomes harder for me
> *(left leg)*
> Life becomes richer in me
> *(bottom line of triangle)*

In its triangular form, one couldn't tell what line came first, so I started with "Life becomes harder for me" which I now know was actually the second line. Given my situation at the time, however, I assumed a slightly different progression of the three sentences: "harder" first, then "clearer," and ending with "richer," which seemed quite appropriately satisfying for the third line even at first reading. So I set off confidently if incorrectly and I soon began to perceive how much peace of soul could be had in a short amount of time. Realizing that exercising and strengthening my inner life would not interfere with my daily life but actually support it made me feel pleasantly smug with relief.

Eventually I saw the three-line verse as Steiner had given it and I had a pleasing wrestle with the first two lines trying to discover whether its new and correct version made significant differences. Ultimately, I found that Steiner used the three-line verse in a lecture given to eurythmy students as part of a fourteen-line verse, printed below. I now use that one rarely but with appreciation for its complexities—part of the "richer in me" that all parts of the verse now offer me—but more often I still treat the "Life becomes" sentences as a separate verse and it still shows me new things.

Steiner's presentation consists not of a meditation but of movements that he asks the eurythmists to make to the fourteen-line spoken verse. "Life becomes" is the final three-line section.

Note: The first four lines constitute a "peace dance." The antiphonal set of eight lines that comes next is the "I-and-you" exercise in Steiner's Directions. The final three lines constitute the triangular verse my mother wrote out and sent to me to contemplate.

✿

Steiner's Directions

Those who took part on the stage yesterday [July 7, 1924] in the interwoven "Peace Dance" and "I and You" exercise will remember how the four groups of three people were arranged; I shall now ask those who were on the stage yesterday to come up again and take these same places.*

Wishes of the soul are quickened,
Deeds of will wax and grow,
Fruits of life are ripening.

I feel my fate,
My fate finds me.
I feel my star
My star finds me.
I feel my aims,
My aims find me.
My soul and the world
Are one.

Life becomes clearer round me,
Life becomes heavier for me,
Life becomes richer in me.

---

* "Peace Dance" and "I and you" refer respectively to the last three lines of the entire verse, the "life becomes" lines, and the middle section of the verse, which has an antiphonal structure of three two-line sets and a final two-line summary, "My soul and the world / Are one" for the middle section (Steiner, *Eurythmy as Visible Speech*, lecture 13).

Here at the same time, I have given you an example of the intimate relationship existing between the language of eurythmy and the language we ordinarily use.

I have attempted—it is naturally only a slight attempt and intended merely as an illustration—to answer the question: "How did poems arise in certain mystery centers where an art of movement existed such as we are endeavoring to renew in eurythmy?" In those centers it was not the language, the structure and form of language in a poem, that had primacy.... It was out of the form, out of the gesture, that the structure of the verse was sought. The eurythmy forms and gestures preceded the fashioning of the verse.

3

The Six Essential Exercises

GRH: Some excellent meditators have chosen to write about Steiner's "six exercises." I think of Michael Lipson's original and graceful version of them in his *Stairway of Surprise* and Florin Lowndes's book *Enlivening the Chakras of the Heart*. Below, I have chosen Steiner's description of the exercises from *Esoteric Science*, occasionally using differences found in *Start Now!*

By following Steiner's descriptions, you will see how the exercises create objectivity in thought, will, and feeling and how the order in which the five individual qualities are to be practiced builds essential values for both inner and outer soul-life. The first time I ventured to do the six exercises—one per month as people thought, in those days, that it had to be done—it took me a whole year to finish. Often I had to start again and repeat most of a month because I had failed to perform the little gesture I had decided would be my daily thing-to-do each morning at a certain hour for the "will month" (turn my wedding ring). Alternatively, I would fail to refrain from expressing laughter at a joke or anger at an injustice in the "equanimity month."

Thirty years old and a mother of four children (then aged six, five, three and one), I had become so absorbed in their beings, needs, and personalities that I had stopped attending to myself. Like many mothers, I realized that intense mothering had kept me from minding my own selfhood and paying specific attention to its development. Doing these essential exercises is invisible and takes almost no time, yet it wakens you to your own being and its consciousness. I needed to attend more consciously to my own interests, shortcomings, and abilities and the exercises do precisely that. Making them my private project, I soon found that it brought insight and substance to me and thus to all of us.

The six exercises are to be performed *in the order that Steiner gives them*. Each of them creates and supports your capacity for objectivity regarding:

- your own thinking,
- your will,
- your inner life of feeling,
- your view of life in general, and
- your willingness to be open to whatever you encounter.

As I ventured forth, my involvement in the demands of the exercises began to bring me a sense of their deep reach for strengthening your soul's insights. Steiner has a winning tone—both serious and matter of fact—and his message is clear the first time you read it, even before you have tried to do it. Later, when the exercises are familiar because you have lived and worked with them, you find yourself nodding your head over their sheer truth and worth when you reread the far-reaching exercises. They not only train our capacities but also reveal to ourselves our inner depths and potentials as human beings.

※

Steiner's Directions and Descriptions for the Six Essential Exercises:

What our thinking needs most of all for spiritual training is objectivity. In this regard, life is the great teacher of the human "I" in the physical world of the senses. If the soul chose to allow its thoughts to wander aimlessly, life would correct it immediately so as to avoid a conflict, for the soul's thinking must correspond to the actual course of life's realities. When, however, we turn our attention away from the physical world of the senses, we are no longer subject to its automatic corrections, so our thinking will go astray if it is not able to correct itself. This is why students of the spirit have to train their thinking so that it can set its own directions and goals. Their thinking must teach itself inner stability and the ability to stick strictly to one subject. For this reason, the appropriate thought exercises we undertake should not deal with unfamiliar and complicated objects, but with ones that are simple and familiar.

1. Over a matter of months, if we can overcome ourselves to the point of being able to focus our thoughts for at least five minutes a day on some ordinary object (for example a pin, a pencil, or the like), and if, during this time, we exclude all thoughts unrelated to this object, we will have made a big step in the right direction. (We can consider a new object each day or stay with the same one for several days.) Even those who consider themselves thinkers because of their scientific education should not scorn this means of preparing themselves for spiritual training, because if we fix thoughts on something very familiar for a certain period of time, we can be certain that we are thinking objectively. If we ask: What is a pencil made of? How are these materials prepared? How are they put together to make pencils? When were pencils invented? and so on, our thoughts correspond to reality much more closely than if we think about the origin of human beings or the nature of life.

Simple thought exercises are better for developing objective thinking about the Saturn, Sun, and Moon phases of evolution than any complicated scholarly ideas, because what we think about is not the point, at least initially. The point is to think objectively, using our own inner strength. Once we have taught ourselves objectivity by practicing on sense-perceptible, physical processes that are easily surveyed, our thinking becomes accustomed to striving for objectivity even when it does not feel constrained by the physical world of the senses and its laws. We break ourselves of the habit of allowing our thoughts to wander without regard for the facts.

2. The soul must become a ruler in the domain of the will just as it is in the world of thoughts. Here again life itself appears as the controlling element in the physical world of the senses. It makes us need certain things, and our will feels roused to satisfy these needs. For the sake of higher training, we must get used to obeying strictly our own commands. If we do this, we will become less and less inclined to desire nonessentials. Dissatisfaction and instability in our life of will, however, are based on desiring things without having any clear concept of realizing these desires. Such dissatisfaction can disrupt our entire mental life when a higher "I" is trying to emerge from the soul.

A good exercise is to tell ourselves to do something daily at a specific time over a number of months: Today at this particular time I will do *this*. We then gradually become able to determine what to do and when to do it in a way that makes it possible to carry out the action in question with great precision. In this way, we rise above damaging thoughts, such as: "I'd like this, I want to do that," which disregard the feasibility of what we want. In *Faust* Goethe put these words into the mouth of the seer, Manto: "I love whoever longs for the impossible." Goethe himself said (in his *Verses in Prose*), "Living in ideas means treating the impossible as if it were possible." What Goethe and his seer ask, however, can be accomplished only by those who have trained themselves in desiring what is possible in order to be able then to apply their strong will to "impossibilities" in a way that transforms them into possibilities.

3. For the sake of spiritual training, the soul should also acquire a certain degree of composure with regard to the domain of feeling. For this to happen, the soul must master its expressions of joy and sorrow, pleasure and pain. Many prejudices become evident with

regard to this particular quality. We might worry that we would become dull and unreceptive to the world around us if we could not empathize with rejoicing or pain. But that is not the point. The soul should indeed rejoice when there is reason to rejoice, and it should feel pain when something sad happens. It is only meant to master its *expressions* of joy and sorrow, of pleasure and displeasure. With this as our goal we will soon notice that rather than becoming dulled to pleasurable and painful events in our surroundings, the opposite is true. We are becoming more receptive to these things than we were previously. Admittedly, acquiring this character trait requires strict self-observation over a long period of time. We must make sure that we are able to empathize fully with joy and sorrow without losing ourselves and expressing our feelings involuntarily. What we are meant to suppress is not our justified pain, but involuntary weeping; not our abhorrence of a misdeed, but blind rage; not alertness to danger, but fruitless fear, and so on.

Exercises like this are the only way for students of the spirit to acquire the mental tranquility that is needed to prevent the soul from leading a second, unhealthy life, like a shadowy double, alongside the higher "I" when this "I" is born and especially when it begins to be active. Especially with regard to these things it is important not to succumb to self-deception. It can easily seem to some that they already possess a certain equilibrium in ordinary life and do not need this exercise, but in fact it is doubly necessary in such a case. It is quite possible to be calm and composed in confronting things in ordinary life and yet have our suppressed lack of equilibrium assert itself all the more when we ascend into higher worlds. It is essential to realize that for purposes of spiritual training, what we seem to possess already is much less important than systematically practicing what we need to acquire. This sentence is quite correct, regardless of how contradictory it may seem. No matter what life may have taught us, *what we teach ourselves is what serves the purposes of spiritual training.* If life has taught us excitability we need to break that habit, but if it has taught us complacency we need to rouse ourselves through self-education so that our souls' reactions correspond to the impressions they receive. People who cannot laugh at anything have as little control over their lives as people who are constantly provoked to uncontrollable laughter.

4. An additional way of training our thinking and feeling is by acquiring a quality we can call "positivity."... The erroneous, the bad, and the ugly must not prevent the soul from finding the true, the good, and the beautiful wherever they are present. We must not confuse this positivity with being artificially uncritical or arbitrarily closing our eyes to things that are bad, false, or inferior. It is possible to admire a dead animal's beautiful teeth and still see the decaying corpse; the corpse does not prevent us from admiring the beautiful teeth. We cannot consider bad things good and false things true, but we can reach the point where the bad does not prevent us from seeing the good, and errors do not keep us from seeing the truth.

5. Our thinking undergoes a certain maturing process in connection with the will when we attempt never to allow anything we have experienced to deprive us of our unbiased receptivity to new experiences. For students of the spirit, the thought, "I've never thought of that; I don't believe it," should lose its meaning completely. During specific periods of time we should be intent on using every opportunity to learn something new concerning everything and every being. If we are ready and willing to take previously unaccustomed points of view, we can learn from every current of air, every leaf, every babbling baby. Admittedly, it is easy to go too far with regard to this ability. At any given stage in life, we should not disregard all our previous experiences. We should indeed judge what we are experiencing in the present on the basis of past experiences. This belongs on one side of the

scales; on the other side, however, students of the spirit must constantly exert their inclination to experience new things and continue to believe in the possibility that new experiences may contradict old ones.

6. We have now listed five soul qualities that students in a genuine spiritual training need to acquire: control of one's train of thought, mastery of one's will impulses, composure in the face of joy and sorrow, positivity in judging the world, and receptivity in one's attitude toward life. Having spent certain periods of time practicing these qualities consecutively, we will then need to bring them into harmony with each other in our souls. We need to practice them in pairs, or in combinations of three and one at the same time, and so on, in order to bring about this harmony.

※

Methods of spiritual training recommend these exercises because if conscientiously carried out, they not only have the above-mentioned direct effects on students but also affect them in many indirect ways that they need on their path to the spiritual worlds. If we do these exercises enough, we will encounter many shortcomings and errors in our soul life and will discover the necessary means of strengthening and safeguarding the activity of our intellect, our feelings, and our character.... In fact we will notice that these exercises indirectly and gradually bring changes to the soul that did not initially seem inherent in them. For example, after a certain time, people with too little self-confidence will notice that doing these exercises develops the self-confidence they need. The same is true of other soul qualities.*

---

*   Steiner, *Esoteric Science,* pp. 310–317.

Three Plant Meditations

4

Perceiving Growth and Decay

A Soul Exercise in Discerning Subtle Realities

GRH: Steiner shows how the soul responds to processes of growth and decay in the surrounding world. When this exercise of discernment first came to me in my twenties or early thirties, I found that I could test my perceptions of growth and decay where everyday life took me. I could monitor my soul responses to freshness or decaying as I went about my ordinary business—a walk in the park pushing a stroller, buying fruits and vegetables, watering my indoor plants, tossing out bouquets that had faded long enough, waiting in line and discreetly looking at faces and hands of people standing nearby. Such situations offered opportunities to exercise soul discernments comparable to those that Steiner mentions here. At first, your responses may be so subtle you can hardly believe they exist, but as you consciously seek opportunities to focus on things in bloom and other things withering, you become familiar with both situations and you find that your soul can make reliable discernments among the subtle differences between growing and decaying.

※

Steiner Describes the Exercise

The first step is to turn our soul's attention toward processes of life as it buds, grows, and flourishes and toward phenomena connected with withering, fading, and dying away. Wherever we look, these two processes are present together. By their nature they always evoke feeling and thought in us. Normally, however, we do not give ourselves sufficiently to these responses and thoughts in our soul. We rush from one sense impression to the next. Now we consciously and intensively focus our full attention on them. Whenever we perceive a quite definite form of blossoming and flourishing, we banish all else from our souls and, for a short time, dwell on this one impression only.

First we observe as actively and precisely as possible. Then we turn our attention—in complete inner equilibrium—to the feelings coming to life in our souls, and the thoughts arising there. If we find the necessary inner peace and surrender ourselves to what comes to life within us, then after some time we will experience the following: We will notice rising up within us new kinds of feelings and thoughts that we never knew before. The more often we focus our attention first on something growing and flourishing, and then on something withering and dying away, the more lively and active these soul responses will become. Eventually, just as the eyes and ears of our physical organism are formed by natural forces out of inanimate matter, so organs of clairvoyant "seeing" are formed out of the feelings and thoughts that arise in relation to growing and flourishing, withering and dying.

By cultivating our feeling life in this way, we will find that a specific form of feeling comes with processes of growing and becoming, while quite another accompanies those of withering and dying. These forms of response can be described, though only approximately. But each individual who actually goes through the inner experience can attain a complete idea of the forms. Whoever repeatedly directs attention to processes of becoming, flourishing, and blossoming will feel something faintly resembling the sensation we experience as we watch the sunrise. Processes of withering and dying, on the other hand, will produce an experience comparable to what we feel when we watch the slow rise of the moon on the horizon.

Surrendering repeatedly to such feelings, we find a new world opening before us. The soul world or so-called astral plane begins to dawn. Growth and decay are no longer merely facts bringing vague impressions, as they were before. Now, our impressions form definite spiritual lines and figures.... These lines and figures are not arbitrary. Two students at the same level of development will see the same lines and figures associated with the same processes. Just as two healthy people with good eyes both see a round table as round—and neither sees it as rectangular—so, in the presence of a flower, two souls both see the same spiritual form arising....

Once we have advanced to the point where we can see the spiritual forms of what appears physically visible to our outer eyes, then we are not far from the stage of seeing things that have no physical existence at all. Such things, of course, remain completely hidden (or occult) to one who has received no esoteric training.[*]

※

GRH: Steiner continues with two paragraphs that warn against losing oneself in speculation:

We should not try to determine what things mean with the speculative mind, but should let things themselves tell us their meaning. (p. 43)

We must never allow ourselves false thoughts and feelings. Random musings, playful daydreams, the arbitrary ebb and flow of feeling—all these must be banished from the soul. We need not fear that this will make us unfeeling. On the contrary, we will find that only when we regulate our inner life in this way do we become truly rich in feelings and creative in genuine imagination. (p. 44)

---

[*] Steiner, *How To Know Higher Worlds*, pp. 39–42.

5

Visible and Invisible

Seed Meditation

GRH: Steiner leads us to create in thought what will eventually become visible in space. As we perform our observations and visualizations, we accompany them with feelings.

I choose a squash seed, because I know how the growth habit of squash looks—like a horizontally creeping vine. Eventually, floppy flowers will appear among the green leaves and some will turn into the stems of real squashes.

The single tiny seed you are examining feels as if it is made of paper and might blow away. Holding it in your open hand, you probably notice the small but definite mound in the center of the seed and how the seed's edges seem to have been pressed flat, a bit like pastry. When Steiner directs you to imagine that in your other hand you are holding a fake seed, which will never grow into anything, no matter how much it looks like the real seed, I imagine the lush growth of the real seed and the nothingness in the imagined seed. That moment of contrast that Steiner supplies keeps the meditation going. It is my favorite moment in the exercise. As the real seed's greenery grows in my mind, I feel as if I'm following a silent melody that starts nearby.

As for the flame that Steiner mentions at the end: Sometimes it happens, often not. Either way, the exercise has brought me to an inner visualizing and feeling, both of which are capacities that become stronger and more interesting the more I do the exercise.

Steiner's Directions

We place before us a small seed from a plant. Starting with this insignificant thing, the point will be to think the right thoughts intensively and, by means of these thoughts, to develop certain feelings. First, we establish what we are really seeing with our eyes. We describe to ourselves the form, color, and other properties of the seed. Then we ponder the thought: "This seed, if planted in the ground, will grow into a complex plant."

We visualize the plant; we make it present to us and within us. We build it up in our imagination. Then we think: What I am now visualizing in my imagination, forces of earth and light will later draw forth actually from this small seed. But if this were an artificial seed, a copy so perfect that my eyes could not distinguish it from a real seed, then no forces of earth and light would ever be able to draw forth such a plant from it."

If we can clearly form this thought and bring it to life within us, then we will be able to form the next thought easily and with the right feeling: "Already concealed within this seed—as the force of the whole plant—lies what will later grow out of it. An artificial copy of the seed has no such force. Yet, to my eyes, both seeds look the same. Therefore, the real seed contains something *in*visible that is absent from the copy."

Thoughts and feelings should now focus on this *in*visible reality. We imagine that this invisible force or reality will in the course of time change into the visible plant, whose color and form will be visible to us. We hold the thought: "The invisible will become visible. If I were unable to think, then what later becomes visible could not announce itself to me now."

It is important to emphasize that whatever we think we must also feel with intensity. Meditative thoughts need to be experienced calmly and peacefully. No other thoughts should distract us and time should be allowed for both the thought and the feeling united with it to penetrate the soul.

If the exercise is done in the right way, then after a time—perhaps only after many unsuccessful attempts—we become conscious of a new force within us. The new force creates a new perception: The seed seems to be enclosed in a small cloud of light. In a sensory-spiritual way, we sense it as a kind of flame. At its center we experience a sensation similar to the impression made by the color purple, at its edges a sensation similar to the color blue.*

❋

GRH: It is not necessary to bring yourself to a spiritual sensing of the flame-like presence in the visible seed. Even if you take the exercise only as far as acknowledging to yourself that you have been able to imagine the visible plant in detail while you concentrate on the visible seed, you will have accomplished much. You will have experienced your capacity to picture the plant that can come from the real seed and cannot come from an imitation one, and the added complexity of the comparison will have brought increased strength to your thinking and feeling.

---

*   Steiner, *How to Know Higher Worlds,* p. 55.

6

Plant Meditation

An Exercise in Nurturing the Capacity for Perception

GRH: Like the "seed meditation" and the "growth and decay" meditation, this exercise also considers what is not visible but will be at a later moment. This meditation, however, begins with the mature, visible plant. Steiner gives directions for noticing the subtle responses we have in our thoughts and feelings when we open our attention to a growing plant, or to a decaying one. Such efforts, he says, develop in the soul a new understanding that a capacity for perceiving spirit realities exists in us. Just as with the other two exercises, this meditation works with not seeing, yet with active feeling and connecting that feeling with a thought, thus creating changes in the soul that can be cultivated over time. The exercises are closely alike. That makes it worth doing all three.

❋

Steiner Describes How to Strengthen the Soul's Thoughts and Perceptions

We place before us a mature plant. First, we immerse ourselves in the thought: "A time will come when this plant will wither and decay. Everything I see now will then no longer exist, but the plant will have produced seeds and these will become new plants. Thus once again I become aware that something I cannot see lies hidden in what I can see." We saturate ourselves with the thought, "The plant form with all its colors will soon no longer be there. But the knowledge that the plant produces seeds teaches me that it will not disappear into nothing-ness. I cannot see what preserves the plant from disappearance just as I do not see the future plant in the seed. Therefore there must be something in the plant, too, that I cannot see with my eyes. But if I let this thought live within me, and the appropriate feeling unites with it, then after a time a new force will grow in my soul and become a new perception."

A kind of spiritual flame form will then grow out of the plant. Of course, this flame will be correspondingly larger than the one described in the case of the seed. The flame will be felt as green-blue at its center and as yellow-red at its periphery. It must be strongly emphasized that we do not see what are here called "col-ors" in the same way that we see colors with our physical eyes. Rather through spiritual perception we experience something similar to the impression made by physical colors. To perceive "blue" spiritually is to feel or sense an impression similar to the one we feel when our physical eyes dwell on the color blue. We have to remember this if we want to ascend gradually to true spir-itual perception. Otherwise, we will expect the spiritual world to be a mere replica of the physical world and that assumption can only lead to the bitterest deception. [Steiner warns of this mistake throughout his lectures and writings.]

Once we have reached the point of true, not fantasized, spiri-tual seeing, we have already achieved much. Things now reveal to us not only their present being but also their arising and passing away. We begin to see the spirit—of which our physical eyes know nothing—everywhere. We have begun to approach the mystery of birth and death with our own intuitive vision.... For the spirit, birth and death are transformations, just as the unfolding of a blossom from the bud is a transformation occurring before our physical eyes. To come to know the spiritual counterpart through our own spiritual vision, we have first to awaken spiritual senses for it in the way indicated here.*

---

*   Steiner, *How To Know Higher Worlds,* p. 59.

Three Meditations on the Cosmos

7

Trust in Thinking

The Thinking Soul and Meditation

*In thinking, I experience myself
united with the stream of cosmic existence.*

GRH—My problem with this aphorism: Until recently I was unable to meditate this aphorism for the simple reason that I couldn't remember it. That showed me I couldn't understand it. Somehow I could not recall the first seven words of this short sentence. Consequently, I kept starting wrong and not finding my way to the end, as though I had turned the wrong way out of an unfamiliar driveway and thus was instantly lost and didn't yet know it. "In thinking I unite myself..." No. Not it. "In thinking I feel united with cosmic streaming..." No. Not it.

Blurring the form of the sentence's beginning, I could not understand the sentence as a whole. Without grasping "I experience myself united with..." as the first event, I missed the rest, too. In order to reach the surface of the sentence, I had to slow down, like this: I am doing something particular when I am thinking. What is that? Yes, I am uniting with the stream of cosmic thinking. No, with the stream of cosmic something. Ah, with the stream of cosmic existence! Yes. "Existence" is what I am uniting with—cosmic existence.

"In thinking I unite..." No: I am not uniting, I experience myself united with... At last: "I feel united with the stream of cosmic existence when I think" That is a form of the actual sentence. "My thinking leads me to a cosmic existence with which I can or do or must unite." Okay, now I have "penetrated" the sentence, as

Steiner puts it. I can grasp it and let its spiritual meanings dawn on me in whatever ways they might come.

What was the obstacle that kept me from hearing the sentence? For me, the sentence crumbled instead of cohering, because I had unconsciously failed to accept one of its basic points—that thinking can be social not only solitary. Thinking is my favorite soul activity and I knew that I do trust it; but I unconsciously resisted the idea that "feeling myself united with" something could be a trustworthy situation in one's thinking. Further, I knew streaming in connection with thinking but not cosmic streaming, and not a streaming of cosmic existence.

I have a warm relationship with this aphorism now. I feel vividly its spiritual strength when, in meditating the sentence, I feel my soul experiencing its thinking and the streaming of cosmic existence as—paradoxically—one.

⁂

Rudolf Steiner on the Paradox of Thinking: An Aphorism

The soul trusts naturally in thinking. Without this trust, the soul would lose all certainty in life. Once we begin to doubt thinking, healthy soul life stops. Thinkers who doubt the validity and power of thinking forget that, after all, doubts and perplexities are themselves results of their thinking activity. If you develop a feeling of trust in relation to thinking, you will find that thinking contains not only something that you form inwardly as the power of the human soul, but also a power that is independent of both you and your soul and that bears within it a cosmic existence. *Your own power to think belongs not only to you but to a world that is independent of you. In discovering your thinking's twofold existence, you are realizing a paradoxical fact: Thinking belongs to you yourself and also participates in a universal existence* [emphasis added].

What you may formerly have been perceiving as private, even isolating, now also has a social, even a cosmic, dimension. There is something deeply calming in being able to surrender oneself to the larger connections of thought life. The soul feels it can get away from itself. It needs this experience just as much as it needs to be able to be completely within itself.

Oscillating between the two keeps the soul life healthy just as losing ourself in sleep for awhile rests us from the confines and stresses of waking life.

Meditating the Aphorism

A good preparation for understanding spiritual insights is to feel frequently what strength lies in the mood or attitude of soul when one meditates the thought,

> *In thinking, I experience myself*
> *united with the stream of cosmic existence.*

The value of meditating this thought lies much less in the abstract understanding of it than in what is to be gained by repeatedly experiencing the strengthening effect it has on the soul. If it flows powerfully through one's inner life, it expands in the soul like a deep spiritual breath of life. Far more than cognizing the content of such a thought, *experiencing* it is what matters. Let the thought be present only *once* in your soul with sufficient conviction, and you can understand it. But if it is to produce further understandings of spiritual facts and spiritual existence, then, when you have understood the sentence, bring it to life again in your soul.

Again and again, fill your soul with the same thought. Let only that thought fill your soul, excluding all other thoughts, feelings, and memories. Repeatedly concentrating on a thought that one has completely penetrated gathers the forces of the soul—forces that in normal life are scattered. The soul strengthens itself—in itself—*and the powers that have been gathered together become organs of perception for the spiritual world and its truths* [emphasis added].

This brief description indicates the right way to proceed in meditation. First, you work your way through to grasping a thought that you can fully understand with the means provided by everyday life and ordinary thinking. Then you sink yourself repeatedly into that thought, become absorbed in it, and make yourself wholly one with it. By living with a thought known in this way, your soul gains strength. Here a thought about the nature of thinking itself was chosen as an example, because it is particularly fruitful for meditation. But what was said about meditation applies to every thought that we thoroughly penetrate.

Steiner's Wise Closing Paragraph on the Mood that Oscillation Brings to Meditation in General

It is especially fruitful for a meditator to know the mood of soul that results from the *pendulum-like oscillating of soul life described above* [emphasis added]. It is the surest way to come to the feeling in your meditation that the spiritual world has touched you directly.

This feeling is a healthy consequence of meditation. It should radiate its strength into everything you do during the rest of your waking day. But it should not be a continuous, ever-present prolongation of the meditative state. Rather, you should feel, *Strength flows into my life from my meditation experience....* The true fruits of meditation are brought to maturity only when we raise our meditation and meditative state above the rest of life. Meditation will have the best effect upon our lives when we experience it to be something special, something uplifting."*

---

*   Steiner, *A Way of Self-Knowledge,* part 1, "The Threshold of the Spiritual World," Aphorism One, "Trust in Thinking," pp. 5–10.

8

Rainbow Colors Exercise

GRH: In 1981, I inherited, among other papers, a homemade New Year's greeting card that had been sent to my mother in 1967. It came from her friends, Hans and Ruth Pusch. Ruth was known for her translations of Rudolf Steiner's works, and Hans for his productions of Steiner's *Four Mystery Dramas*, written between 1910 and 1913: "The Portal of Initiation"; "The Soul's Probation"; "The Guardian of the Threshold"; and "The Souls' Awakening." The 1967 greeting card was actually a little booklet of colored pages (8.5 x 5.5 inches), stacked and then folded in half and tied at the centerfold. The pages were arranged in rainbow order, with red for the beginning and end, and violet at the center. On the first seven little left-hand pages, Hans Pusch recalled how he had been delighted to hear Steiner giving his lecture cycle on speech and drama (Sept. 18, 1924). He was particularly moved by Steiner's words in lecture 14 about developing sensitivity for "the language of color as expression of character in costumes, of mood and atmosphere in lighting and stage décor."

On each rainbow-colored page of the booklet's second half, Hans and Ruth Pusch had typed a short, revelatory characterization that Steiner had given about the color of that page, adapting it slightly but not interpreting or otherwise differing fundamentally from Steiner's lecture. Quoting, almost verbatim, Steiner's descriptions of each rainbow color on its particular page, the Pusches had introduced an intimate feeling for the colors by speaking to each one as "you" and addressing it by its name. The words you read below are Steiner's, but the rhetoric of direct address (added by the Pusches) brings Steiner's words even closer to the soul when we work with the colors meditatively. I have also included excerpts from the Pusches' introductory reminiscences of Steiner's lecture on the rainbow colors.

I began to meditate the rainbow colors in January 1982, using the Pusches' form of Steiner's rich characterizations for each color, sometimes as a concentration exercise with a single color, sometimes as the main course of my meditation menu for that day. The descriptions bring you "face to face with the soul and spirit that is in nature." The mood of the reminiscences lets the "eye of soul" connect directly with the rainbow colors themselves. As you address each color in turn and begin to feel at one with it, you experience your soul receiving the color's specific gift in a conscious, soul-spiritual way. I have done the Rainbow Colors Exercise almost every January since 1982 and found it a fitting accompaniment to January's twofold glance—backward over Christmas nights and forward toward the next year's unfolding.

※

A Description by Hans and Ruth Pusch

The September days of 1924—forty-two years ago—stand out in the memory of those who witnessed them. Rudolf Steiner gave seventy lectures within three weeks to the friends assembled in Dornach: to members in general, to physicians and priests, actors, and workers. Outwardly, they were hot summer days; inwardly, days of spirit fire in the Pentecostal sense of the word.... One of the main subjects in those weeks was the renewal of the dramatic art out of the source from which it sprang: mystery centers.

In lecture 14 of *Speech and Drama*, Steiner recommends developing a new sensitivity for the language of color, as expression of character in costumes, of mood and atmosphere in lighting and stage décor. Rudolf Steiner showed how such a color experience can be achieved. He recommended our looking at the rainbow whenever its phenomenon appears in nature. He sketched the way the human soul can become one with the different moods displayed there in heavenly transparency.

Remembering the modulation of his voice, the translation here offered tries to capture the rhapsodic mood in which the words were spoken. They carried the listener into spheres of soul and spirit.*

When I look at you
v i o l e t
shining out
further and further
into immeasurable distances,
I am impelled to pray.

In you, b l u e
I can rest, permeated
by the quiet mood
which streams from you.

And it is as if I had left
the gods, to whom I looked up
in awe through the violet-blue
when now I approach
the g r e e n arch.

Through you, g r e e n,
I pour myself out
into everything that grows,
sprouts and blossoms.
You g r e e n
open the door
to a perceptive sympathy
and antipathy with all
that is around me.

---

* Ruth and Hans Pusch, "For the New Year, 1967."

Taking into myself
the rainbow g r e e n
I begin to understand
all the beings and things
of the world.

You y e l l o w
strengthen me that I may
live within myself,
inwardly affirming:
I am humanity;
I am more than nature;
I am allowed to be human
with nature surrounding me.

And inner warmth reveals
To me my own essence:
You o r a n g e
make me sensible of
the character—
with all its virtues
and its shortcomings—
that is revealed
in this warmth of mine.

You r e d
lead me out again into the realm
whence the shining violet came
awakening such pious feelings.
Now my inner being responds
and calls forth what lives
within it
of overflowing joy
of enspirited courage to sacrifice,
of love for all humanity.[*]

---

[*]   Verse from Steiner, *Speech and Drama,* lecture 14, Sept. 18, 1924.

Alas! Human beings see but the body of the rainbow. When with the eye of soul we behold its colors, we are not looking at nature merely in her outer aspect; we are face to face with the soul and spirit that is in nature.[*]

---

[*]   Pusch, "For the New Year, 1967."

9

From Static to Dynamic

The Triangle Exercise

GRH—An introductory note on Nominalism and Realism: The triangle exercise asks what a triangle is in its universal essence. By imagining a flood of triangles pulsing forth in motion rather than as finished, static shapes each of which is labeled "triangle," Steiner frames the exercise in the context of the great dispute between Nominalists and Realists in the twelfth and thirteenth centuries, the time of Thomas Aquinas (1225–1271). For Aquinas and the other Scholastics, including Albertus Magnus, what they called "universals" are real and perceptible sources of manifestations. However, for Nominalists "universals" were merely the names that labeled things, not the sources of things. Only the sensory world existed for the Nominalists. Their naming was based on sensory perception not on experiences of essences or cosmic activities. Whereas Realists perceived universals as higher realities capable of manifesting in the sensory world, for Nominalists cosmic facts did not exist.

Putting the Triangle Exercise in the context of the disputes and mistakes regarding Nominalism and Realism lets Steiner lead up to the question, "Which of all the various triangles I can draw is the real triangle, the essential one?" With this question, the triangle exercise places the Realist–Nominalist conflict in relation to the problem of whether human thinking can manage to cognize non-material things. Can human beings think cosmically? Can our thinking recognize that suprasensory sources create the manifesting sensory world? In short, can our thinking learn to contemplate and cognize spiritual realities or must it confine itself to physical ones?

Steiner frames the entire exercise in a description of the Nominalist-versus-Realist conflict, because Nominalist prejudice remained a potential obstacle in his time, as it does in ours, preventing people from being able to perceive and perform Anthroposophy as a Spiritual Science and work with it accordingly. In doing the triangle exercise ("again and again" as Steiner so often says regarding meditative work) we can practice overcoming what Owen Barfield calls our "residual Nominalism." The Nominalist mentality cannot cognize human identity as an essence, only as an abstraction or label. Nominalist cognizing dismisses the findings of Steiner's Anthroposophy and believes its other name, "spirit science," to be an oxymoron. But thanks to the consciousness soul's link to our selfhood, we can feel our selfhood as both physical and spiritual. Such encounters with our "I" we recognize as real. In short, by means of exercises like those that Steiner gave, we overcome the lazy prejudices of anti-Realism and discover the Realist in us. (For further examples, see Steiner's *Redemption of Thinking*, p. 84, and part two of Steiner's *Riddles of Philosophy*, especially pp. 466–468.)

※

Steiner Describes How to Proceed with the Exercise

The development of thought leads to a stage of doubting the existence of what are called "universals," general concepts, and thus leads to so-called Nominalism, the view that universals can be no more than "names," nothing but words. And this view is still widely held today.

In order to make this clear, let us take a general concept that is easily observable—the concept "triangle." Now anyone still in

the grip of Nominalism of the eleventh to the thirteenth centuries will say somewhat as follows: "Draw me a triangle!" Good!
I draw a triangle for him.... "Right!" says he. "That is a quite
specific triangle with three acute angles. But I will draw another
with an obtuse angle." And he draws a right-angled triangle, and
another with an obtuse angle....

Then, says the person in question, "Well, now we have an
acute-angled triangle, a right-angled triangle, and an obtuse-
angled triangle. They certainly exist, but they are not *the* triangle.
The collective or general triangle must contain every form that a
triangle can have. But a triangle that is acute-angled cannot be at
the same time right-angled and obtuse-angled. Hence there cannot be a collective triangle"*....

At first it seems hopeless to think of drawing a triangle that
would contain all characteristics, all triangles.... [However]
there is a possibility of passing beyond the boundary.... Let us
take this triangle that we have here, and let us allow each side to
move as it will in any direction and moreover we allow it to move
with varying speeds.... We arrive at the uncomfortable notion of
saying: I will not only draw a triangle and let it stay as it is, but I
will make certain demands on your imagination. You must think
to yourself that the sides of the triangles are in continual motion.
The universal or general one cannot be captured in a drawing.
The universal one is of a different order from the ones you have
drawn, yet it is still "triangle." The point of the exercise is to
bring yourself to this boundary and realize that your thinking
can cross it, but only if you work imaginatively.

In this case it is not quite so easy; we have to carry our
movements in our thought. But in this way we really do lay hold
of the triangle in its general form; we fail to get there only if we
are content with *one* triangle. The general thought "triangle" is

---

* There is no word that refers to all possible triangles and one
  cannot draw a composite triangle. —GRH

there if we keep the thought in continual movement, if we *make it* versatile.*

⁂

GRH—Summarizing the goal of the exercise: You will find that you have to stop drawing particular triangles if you want to come to a universal or general triangle. Your goal is to imagine triangles as endless versions of what triangles share. What they share is not an image, not even a rule. Rather they share a moving, generating relationship from which specific triangles can manifest.

Using only your imagination, you slowly and deliberately build up a triangle one side at a time—three perfectly straight lines any two of which must intersect with the third straight line. Slowly and carefully you imagine the three lines. Then you start changing that triangle by moving each line slowly into a different relation to the other two lines, but always still letting those two lines intersect the line you have moved. You continue—moving another line, and then another, changing the angles each time. Still slowly and carefully, you are now imagining the triangle in motion. Bringing motion into your imagining of triangles gives a fresh quality of aliveness to your mental work. You experience the idea of triangles as a dynamic that lives in any particular triangle one might draw though you wouldn't say that this dynamic itself can be drawn. You realize that the way this "universal" now exists in your mind requires you to enter mentally into movement. You are focusing your attention on this triangular wholeness, this movement that could be called "triangling" or "to triangle" as if it were a verb. You cannot point to it or draw it because it does not exist spatially.

You are engaging a living, generating activity that has a source-like relation to triangles of the sort that can be drawn. Whenever you build up this exercise from imagining yourself drawing some exemplary triangles to imagining that which makes all of the drawn

---

* From Steiner, *Human and Cosmic Thought* (during the Second General Meeting of the Anthroposophical Society), pp. 13ff.

ones part of the group called "to triangle," you always come to the point where you change static into dynamic. Precisely that transformation is what Steiner values in the exercise: the key is to see universals or ideas as fluid movement rather than stagnant molds.

Three Meditations on Moral Ideas

The Rose Cross

Making and Meditating the Mental Image of a Symbol

GRH: The Rose Cross has a central place in Steiner's meditations, just as Rosicrucian mystery wisdom has in his lectures and biography. This classic description of how to go about making the mental image of a symbol and meditating it has three interlocked activities, like a chain. First, he tells how to prepare by constructing the content of the mental image, then how to erase the preparation as mere scaffolding, once the awakened soul is ready to contemplate. After the erasing, we are to focus, as long as possible, on what then remains.

❋

Steiner's Instruction on the Meditation

In our everyday soul life, the soul's concerns and interests are divided among many different things and our mental images shift rapidly. In spiritual training, however, the point is to concentrate the soul's entire activity on a single mental image that is freely chosen as a focus for consciousness.... Symbolic images are better than ones that represent outer objects or processes, since these do not force the soul to rely on itself to the same extent as it does with symbols that it creates out of its own activity. The object of imagination is unimportant. What is important is that the process of visualizing the image frees the soul from dependence on anything physical.

By recalling in memory something we have recently seen, we can begin to grasp what it means to immerse ourselves in a visualized image. For example, if we look at a tree and then turn away from it so that we can no longer see it, we can reawaken the mental image of the tree by means of our memory. The mental image we have of a tree when it is not actually present before our eyes is the *memory* of the tree. Now let us imagine that we retain this memory in our soul; we allow the soul to rest on this memory image, and attempt to exclude all other images. The soul is then immersed in the memory image of the tree. If, however, we attempt the same thing with a mental image that we insert into our consciousness through an act of free will, rather than having first perceived it by our senses, we will gradually be able to achieve the necessary effect.

I will illustrate such an attempt with a single example of contemplating or meditating on a symbolic mental image. First, this mental image must be built up in the soul. I can do this as follows: I imagine a plant taking root in the ground, sprouting one leaf after another, and continuing to develop up to the point of flowering. Now I imagine a human being alongside this plant. In my soul, I bring to life the thought that this human being has qualities and abilities that can be called more perfect than those of the plant. I think about how human beings are able to move around in response to their feelings and intentions, while plants are attached to the ground. Then I also notice that although human beings are certainly more perfect than plants, they also have characteristics whose absence in plants can make plants seem more perfect than humans. Human beings are filled with desires and passions that their actions obey, and certain errors result from these drives and passions. In contrast, I see how plants obey the pure laws of growth as they develop leaf by leaf and open their blossoms passionless to the chaste rays of the sun. I can say that human beings have an advantage over plants with regard to a certain type of perfection but that they have to pay a price for this perfection by letting urges, desires, and passions enter their nature in contrast to the forces of the plants that seem so pure to me.

Next I visualize green sap flowing through the plant and imagine this as an expression of the pure passionless laws of growth; and I visualize how red blood flows through human arteries and is an expression of urges, desires, and passions. I allow all this to arise in my soul as a vivid thought. Then I think about how human beings are capable of development, how they can use their higher soul faculties to cleanse and purify their urges and passions. I think about how this cleansing destroys the baser element in their urges and passions, which are then reborn on a higher level. The blood may then be imagined as the expression of these cleansed and purified urges and passions. In my soul now I look, for example, at a red rose and say: In the red sap of the rose blossom I see the color of the plant's green sap transformed into red; and the red rose, like the green leaf, obeys the pure, passionless laws of growth. Let the red of the rose symbolize human blood that has been stripped of all its urges and passions and is now as pure as the growth forces that are active in the blossoming rose.

Now I try not only to assimilate these thoughts with my intellect but also to bring them to life in my feeling. I can have a blissful sensation when I imagine the growing plant's purity and absence of passion. I can balance this bliss by generating in my soul a solemn feeling of gravity when I think of how we human beings carry in ourselves desires and passions whose baser elements we ourselves must purify before we can develop our potential perfection. A third feeling then stirs in me as I devote myself to the joyous, liberating thought of the red blood which, like the transformed sap of the red rose blossom, can become the bearer of purified inner capacities. As we prepare the symbolic mental image that we intend to meditate, it is important to dwell in thoughts and feelings like those described here. After we have done so, we transform our thoughts and feelings into the following symbolic image:

We imagine a black cross. Let this be the symbol of the baser element that has been eliminated from our urges and passions. At the center of the cross, where the two beams of the cross meet, we imagine seven radiant, red roses arranged in a circle. Let these be the symbol of the blood that expresses [signifies] cleansed, purified passions and desires. We now call up this symbolic mental image before our mind's eye. A symbolic mental image such as this has the power to awaken our souls. We immerse ourselves in it and inwardly devote ourselves to it, trying to exclude all other mental images while we are immersed in this one. We allow only this symbol to hover before our mind's eye—as intensely as possible. The symbol becomes a token alongside the inner feeling that our thoughts and responses have created in our souls.

The effectiveness of the symbol lies in the soul experience it brings us. We stay with this soul experience and mood as long as we can. The longer we can dwell on it without disturbance from a different, disrupting image, the more effective the whole process will be. It is not necessary to build up the mental image of the symbol each time we meditate it. The meditation itself consists of the symbol and the soul mood the symbol creates in us. It is, however, a good idea to repeat frequently—outside the time set for our meditation—the process of constructing the mental image through thoughts and responses like those described, so that the vividness of the symbol does not fade away. The more patiently we renew the mental image, the more significant it becomes for our souls....

A symbol such as the rose cross is not a copy of any outer thing or being that nature has produced. This very fact gives the symbol its soul-awakening power. It could be objected that all the details, the black color, the roses, and so on belong to the sensory world. But what wakens our soul is not these details but how they are combined in preparing for the meditation. The mental image of the rose cross does not depict anything present in nature. In spiritual training manifold images like this one can be used and they can be constructed in various ways. Certain sentences, phrases, or single words may also be taken as subjects for meditation. In all cases, such themes for inner meditation have one aim: to liberate the soul from sense-perception and rouse it to activity in which physical sense impressions have no meaning while using the awakened inner soul faculties becomes essential.*

❋

GRH—An editorial summary with autobiographical comments: Each year during the weeks before Easter I do this meditation and have for many years, sometimes continuing it through Whitsun.

1. Steiner's sequence of preparatory imaginations to accompany the content of the meditation guides our consciousness. For me, in the early years, his preparatory sequence of pictures, moods, and details constituted most of the entire meditation I actually performed. The contrast between plants and human beings was the foundation of my meditation.

2. Once our vivid contemplation of the details has created precise mental images in our soul, along with particular moods, we can leave the preparatory sequence behind and focus on the symbol itself—the rose cross: the black cross with seven red roses in a circle at its center. In the early years, when I came to contemplating the symbol itself, that was where I ended my meditation.

3. When we have focused intensely on the mental image of the symbol for a time, we perform a further activity: We erase the black cross with the seven red roses circling its center. Now our soul-spiritual attention dwells on *what remains in us* from having prepared and then absorbed our

---

* Steiner, *Esoteric Science*, pp. 290ff. Note: I have blended this text slightly with an earlier edition, *Occult Science: An Outline*. I have also used the text in *Start Now!*, pp. 191ff.

consciousness in viewing the symbol. What remains after erasing the picture of the rose cross is our wakened readiness for soul-spiritual perceiving and experiencing. We hold that readiness as an experience as long as we can, with or without further perceiving or inquiry.

In recent years I have become able to integrate this third stage into my contemplation. I knew well how to build it up according to Steiner's priceless descriptions, so I could bring them to mind ready to be erased. I understand the scope and nature of contemplating what remains after erasing the actual symbol, and it has become the central activity of my meditation on this Rosicrucian symbol, but I do still spend time on the well-organized, classic opening Steiner creates for meditating the symbol in context. I return to his contrasting descriptions whenever I feel a need to hear, as it were, the firm, inspiring words and images that Steiner provides for us.

11

Meditating on a Feeling of Joy

GRH—An Introductory Preview. Steiner placed this meditation right after his description of meditating the Rose Cross. He did not give it a title as he had done with the Rose Cross. Here, instead of working with a symbol we work with a feeling—a feeling of satisfaction and joy that has arisen in us when we have witnessed an act of kindness or generosity. As with the Rose Cross meditation, though much more briefly, Steiner indicates how one might build up the situation so that it becomes an example of a moral idea in which the meditating soul can focus on what inspired the deed. What will be effective, Steiner says, is not witnessing the act of goodness but *forming the moral idea that inspired the good deed and focusing on that idea.*

The meditation might start when we see someone doing a deed that clearly comes from her or his heart. Encountering something like that our soul may feel joy and satisfaction, but we erase the situation before us and turn our attention to those joyous feelings in our soul. We allow the original situation to fade and let our soul's sensations work onward in us. A feeling of joy fills our consciousness until we experience it as a continuing feeling growing more and more alive in our soul.

This form of the meditation process allows for two important factors that Steiner sees as fundamental to safe meditative work: One is that a meditation be rooted in physical realities; the other, that it be constructed and conducted to arc towards experiences and perceptions of spiritual realities as vivid and reliable as those we already experience in the physical.

❋

Rudolf Steiner:
Experiencing Good-heartedness in Another Human Being

It is...possible to meditate only on feelings, sensations, and so on, and such meditations prove to be especially effective. Let us take the feeling of joy, for example. In the normal course of our lives, our soul may experience joy when an outer stimulus for it is present. A soul with healthy feelings who sees a person doing something out of the goodness of her or his heart will experience satisfaction and joy. However, such a soul could then proceed to take an action of this sort, saying, "When human beings act out of the goodness of their heart they are acting not out of self-interest but in the interest of their fellow human beings. An action like that can be called morally good." The meditating soul can now free itself completely from its mental image of the individual case in the outer world that has given it joy or satisfaction, and can instead form a comprehensive idea of good-heartedness itself.

Perhaps the meditating soul now thinks of how good-heartedness comes about when one soul absorbs another's interest and makes it its own. The meditating soul can then feel joy in this moral idea of good-heartedness. This joy is not due to any process in the sensory world; it is joy in an *idea* as such.

If we attempt to keep such joy alive in the soul for a certain length of time, we are meditating on a feeling, a sensation. What then becomes effective in arousing our inner soul faculties *is not the idea itself*, but rather the *ongoing influence of a feeling within the soul* [my emphases] that has not been stimulated by a mere individual, outer impression.

[Though] meditating on feelings derived from suprasensory experience is [known to be] much more effective in the developing of soul faculties, ... we should be aware that we can go quite far simply through energetic meditation on feelings and sensations of the sort typified by meditating on good-heartedness.[*]

⁂

GRH—A Review of "Erasing and Replacing": What Steiner described is a situation that originates with sensory experience but is then, through contemplative inquiry and quiet meditation, gradually released into a purely spiritual experience, made purely spiritual by being laundered, as it were, through the contemplative inquiry that produced the idea. That idea is no longer dependent on the outer behavior that was witnessed. Rather, thinking the idea of generosity and free giving has released the sensation of good-heartedness from the outer situation.

As Steiner describes the process, each stage of this meditation gives way to the next one *by erasing* what is being perceived and *by substituting* a new, more subtle perception in its place: First, the witnessing of good-hearted behavior and the feeling of joy and satisfaction in response; second, letting the original scene of kindness give way to a contemplative inquiry about human beings' capacity for selflessness and good-hearted behavior. Changing our focus from the situation to our own contemplative activity yields "a comprehensive idea" about the joyous sensations we are feeling.

The idea we have formed is *now independent* of the situation that brought us to it, and that independence enables us to find a third level of experience: We can now *experience an ongoing perception* of the joyous sensations, but they are *now freed* from both a particular stimulating situation and a constructed idea. Our soul and joy become one for as long as we can sustain that union. Steiner often points to the possibility of reaching such essentially open, subtle, and revelatory stages of receptivity, while at the same time warning that sustaining a meditative

---

[*]   Steiner, *Esoteric Science*, p. 297.

reality of this kind is unlikely to occur until the whole process has been attempted many times and over a long period.

Note: This meditation can be used as a group exercise. To begin with, the group is asked to visualize a good-hearted act they have witnessed. Each person then turns to a single other member of the group and the two of them share their memory of the good-hearted act they once witnessed. After that initial sharing, the meditation proceeds in privacy, as described above by Steiner. Once the private meditation has run its course (perhaps in five minutes), all members of the group are invited to report their own experiences of the meditation to the rest of the group.*

---

*   The group exercise came to me from Ron Dunselman, a leader of Anthroposophy in Holland for many years and a member of the Goetheanum seminar, "Meditation Worldwide" (2004–2007). He introduced this socially sharing version of the good-heartedness exercise to the seminar. We all resolved to bring it to meditation groups in the future. For similar group work, see Lipson, *Group Meditation.*

12

Point and Periphery Exercise

GRH: In lecture 10 (July 5, 1924) of his *Curative Education* course, Rudolf Steiner spoke to a small group of doctors and coworkers about developing confidence and courage for their work with children in need of special care, or "special soul care," as Steiner and the professionals decided to call it. He recommends an exercise that one begins in the evening before going to sleep and completes in the morning once one is fully awake. Not only will this exercise strengthen the student's confidence, he says, but it will also stir in us an intuitive conviction that metamorphosis characterizes the process of development, both "normal" and "abnormal." In a lecture given the next day, Steiner returns to the point and periphery exercise, now under the topic of metamorphosis. It broadens the meditation on point and periphery, center and circumference, to hear both treatments Steiner mentions.

⁂

Steiner's Directions to Doctors and Coworkers Who Work with Children in Need of Special Care

Try to accustom yourselves to live your way every evening into the consciousness, *In me is God.* In me is God—or the spirit of God, or what other expression you prefer to use. (But please do not think I mean just persuading yourself of this truth theoretically—which is what the meditations of the majority of people amount to!) Then, in the morning, let the knowledge *I am in God* shine out over the whole day. Now consider! When you bring to life within you these two ideas, which are then no longer mere thoughts but have become something felt and perceived inwardly (yes, have even become impulses of will within you), what is it you are doing?

blue circle

yellow center

First, you have *this* picture before you: *In me is God* [blue circle, yellow center].... And in the morning you have *this* [lower] picture before you: *I am in God* [yellow circle, blue center]. They are one and the same, the upper and lower figures. Now you must

blue center

yellow circle

understand: Here [lower picture] you have a circle (yellow); here [still in the lower picture] you have a point (blue). It doesn't look like that in the evening, but in the morning the truth comes to light. And in the morning you have to think: *Here* is a circle (blue) [in the upper picture]; here [still in the upper picture] is a point (yellow). Yes, you have to understand that *a circle is a point,* and *a point a circle.* You have to acquire a deep inner understanding of this fact.

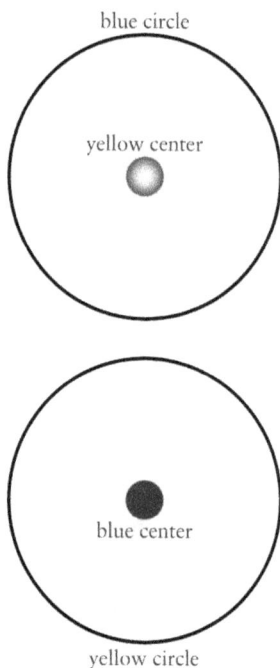

Steiner Returns to the Point and Periphery Exercise of the Previous Day

You will yourselves come to acquire a true insight into...metamorphosis if you continue to practice again and again the meditation I gave you yesterday, when I told you: Here is a circle, here is a point; there the circle is a point, there the point is a circle and so on. Over and over again in your meditation, let the circle steal into the point, let the point expand to the circle. As you do this, you will find that something reveals itself to you, namely, how the metabolism-and-limb organization comes into being out of the head organization. Continue with the meditation until, when you say to yourself, *The point is a point, the circle is a circle,* you are sensible of the *head.* And when you say to yourself, *The point is a circle, the circle is a point*—when, that is, you assert the converse—you discover that you are gliding right down into the *metabolic system....* You will see quite clearly that it is only through this kind of thinking—the kind of thinking called for in Anthroposophy—that we can ever hope to attain insight into the nature of the defects in children with developmental difficulties. This is what we have been attempting in these lectures.*

---

* From Steiner, *Education for Special Needs,* pp. 177–178; and pp. 201–202.

13

The Foundation Stone Meditation

GRH: The Foundation Stone meditation is the *Ecce Homo* of Anthroposophy. My mother introduced the verse to me at Christmas when I was almost twenty-six years old and my father had died suddenly in November over the Thanksgiving weekend. They had both discovered Anthroposophy when they were courting and their continuous conversation brought Anthroposophy into our house and sent their three daughters, including me, to the New York Rudolf Steiner School. Sitting shoulder to shoulder and thigh to thigh on the living room sofa in front of the fireplace, my mother and I read the verse in German, while she translated it into English as we went along. It was clear, though unspoken, that our reading and translating as we sat together was a Christmas gift in which my father was participating.

I meditate the Foundation Stone verse every year during the Advent weeks before Christmas, when autumn gives way to winter (in New England) and a holy time is coming, when mysteries of heart and soul reveal their open secrets to open souls and minds. Then during the twelve or thirteen holy nights of Christmas itself, I meditate the "rhythms," those brief repeats lifted out of the verses, free of syntax, more like an intimate nod than a long gaze at the complicated details of the entire verse. Steiner used the "rhythms" one per day during the week of the 1923–24 Christmas reconstituting of the Anthroposophical Society.

All of Steiner's verses and insights support, and are supported by, his esoteric yet publicly available writings and lectures. The same is true of the Foundation Stone meditation. Like so many of

Steiner's verses the Foundation Stone has a firm architecture that lets you read and meditate it as though you are working with a piece of music or beholding a painting you've known and studied for a long time. The Foundation Stone meditation is as much a great work of art as is the true human being itself. In its architecture we can find the threefold human being as body, soul, and spirit. In the prayer-like last part we feel how intimately human beings belong to the cosmos and how we can give our soulful hearts and heads to the good will of the world, warmed and illumined by our lives.

In *Start Now!*, a book of collected meditations, verses, and exercises by Rudolf Steiner, Christopher Bamford writes a portrait of the "Foundation Stone Meditation" in his introduction to the verses:

> At the center of Anthroposophy, as its lifeblood and heart, lies this meditation, which Rudolf Steiner laid "in the heart of the members" at the first meeting of the reconstituted General Anthroposophical Society during the Holy Nights of 1923–24. It represents the seed and the fruit of anthroposophic striving—the seed, because meditating upon it develops the full and glorious being of Anthroposophia; the fruit, because it is the culmination of Steiner's spiritual work. (p. 239)

※

Foundation Stone Meditation

*Given by Rudolf Steiner at the Refounding
of the Anthroposophical Society, Dornach,
Switzerland, Christmas 1923–24*

Human Soul!
You live in the limbs
that carry you through the realm of space
into spirit's oceanic being.
Practice spirit remembering
in the soul's depths,
where, in the powerful world-creator's being
your "I" gains being in the "I" of God;
then you will truly *live*
in humanity's cosmic being.

For the Father spirit of the heights reigns
in world depths, begetting being.

Spirits of Power!
Let there echo in the depths
What sounds forth from the heights
saying: *"Humanity's being is born from the Divine."*
Spirits hear it in east, west, north, south.
May human beings hear it!

Human soul!
You live in the beat of heart and lung,
which leads you through time's rhythm
into the feeling of your own soul's being.
Practice spirit mindfulness
in balance of soul,
where surging deeds of world becoming
unite your own "I"
with the cosmic "I";
then you will truly *feel*
in human soul-making.

For the Christ will reigns
in circumference,
in world-rhythms, gracing souls.

Spirits of Light!
Let what is formed in the west
be kindled from the east
saying: *In Christ, death becomes life.*

Spirits hear it in east, west, north, south.
May human beings hear it!

Human Soul!
You live in the quiet head,
where from eternal foundations
cosmic thoughts unveil before you.
Practice spirit beholding
in peace of thought
where the eternal aims of gods
shed cosmic being's light
upon your innermost "I"
for your free willing;
then you will truly *think*
in humanity's spirit foundations.

For Spirit's cosmic thoughts reign
in cosmic being, beseeching light.

Spirits of Soul!
Let there be sought in the depths
what is heard in the heights
saying: *the soul awakens through Spirit's cosmic
     thinking.*
Spirits hear it in east, west, north, south.
May human beings hear it!

At the turn of time,
The spirit light of the cosmos descended
into Earth's stream of being.
Reign of night was over;
day-bright light
poured into human souls—
light that warms poor shepherds' simple hearts,
light that illumines the wise heads of kings.

Divine light,
Christ Sun,
warm our hearts,
illumine our heads
so that, what we
from our warm hearts and guided heads
want earnestly to accomplish,
may
be
good.*

❋

---

* The "Foundation Stone Meditation" is my translation, melded
with Christopher Bamford's in *Start Now!*, pp. 239–242. —GRH

Foundation Stone Rhythms

12/26/1923 (Wednesday)

Practice spirit remembering
Your "I" gains being in the "I" of God

Practice spirit mindfulness
Unite your own "I" with the cosmic "I"

Practice spirit beholding
World being's light upon your innermost "I"

12/27/1923 (Thursday)

Your I gains being
in God's "I"

Live
in humanity's cosmic being

Your I unites
with the world's "I"

Feel
in human soul-making

shed cosmic being's light
for your free willing
on your innermost "I"

Think
in humanity's spirit foundations

12/28/1923 (Friday)

Practice spirit remembering
for the father spirit of the heights
　　reigns in cosmic depths
begetting life

Practice spirit mindfulness
for the Christ-will reigns in circumference,
　　in cosmic rhythms
gracing souls

Practice spirit vision
for the cosmic spirit thoughts reign in cosmic being
craving light

12/29/1923 (Saturday)

Practice spirit remembering
Seraphim
Cherubim
Throne
Let from the heights resound
What echoes in the depths

Practice spirit mindfulness
Dominions
Mights
Powers
Let there be kindled from the East
What is formed in the West

Practice spirit vision
Archai
Arc-angels
Angels
Let there be prayed in the depths
What may be heard in the heights

12/30/1923 (Sunday)

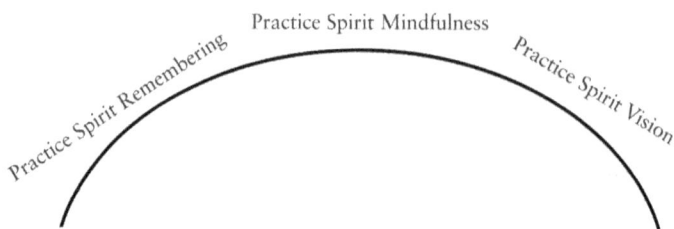

Practice Spirit Mindfulness

Practice Spirit Remembering

Practice Spirit Vision

That what we,
From the bottom of our hearts, from our heads
Earnestly want to accomplish
May
Be
Good

12/31/1923 (Monday)

Divine light
Christ Sun
Spirits hear it in east, west, north, south
May human beings hear it

1/1/1924 (Tuesday)

You live in the limbs
For the father spirit reigns in the heights, in the depths
Begetting being

You live in the beat of heart and lung
For the Christ-will reigns in circumference, in cosmic
    rhythms
Gracing souls

You live in the quiet head
For the spirit's cosmic thinking reigns in cosmic being
Seeking light

Afterword:
Fostering Transformations from the Future

W e are brought once again to the "I," this time by combining Anthroposophy with renewal of religion. It brings new mysteries for humans' meditative engagement with the "I" in the time of the consciousness soul. The meditative "I" can foster what the Christ brings to all of the heavens and the earth in transformations from the future, beginning in our time with the transformation of the astral body into spirit self, made possible by adding the spirit soul to the earlier soul formations—namely the "sentient soul" and the "intellectual soul."

Grail Knowledge: "The New Initiation Knowledge with the Christ Mystery as Its Center"*

What Steiner calls "Grail Knowledge" refers to the question Parcival first failed to ask and then, after journeying farther, finally spoke, "What ails thee?" At first, Grail Knowledge was "hidden knowledge" for the most part, because the old ways of knowing were making room, however, for the new ones that, just because they were new in the fourth and later the fifth post-Atlantis epoch, were not yet fully established. The "remnant of the ancient, dusk-like suprasensory consciousness that all of humankind had formerly possessed"** no longer delivered suprasensory knowledge in dreams, yet the new consciousness had not yet dawned until the "consciousness soul" era of the fifth and

---

* Steiner, *Esoteric Science,* p. 388.
** Ibid., p. 384.

sixth epochs, beginning in 1500 CE. Nevertheless, in the fourth epoch "there were...individuals who quite consciously began to develop...higher powers"* that made it possible for them to break through into the world of soul and spirit again. These powers would be developed more fully after the beginning of the consciousness soul time when they would enable meditations like the ones Steiner's Anthroposophy offers in this handbook so that meditating can train soul faculties to

> experience...higher realms of existence *through their own imagination, inspiration, and intuition.*... The path to suprasensory worlds whose first stages have been described in this book leads to "the science of the Grail.".... To the extent that human evolution will absorb Grail Knowledge, the impulse supplied by the Christ event can become ever more significant. Increasingly, an inner aspect will be added to the external aspect of Christian evolution. What we can recognize through imagination, inspiration, and intuition about the higher worlds *in conjunction with the Christ Mystery* will increasingly permeate our life of ideas, feeling, and will. 'Hidden' Grail knowledge will become evident; as an inner force, it will increasingly permeate the manifestations of human life.**

Clearly and very seriously, Steiner's words about the Grail Knowledge tell readers that Christ has *supplied* the impulse of his eternal presence. "Supplied the impulse of his eternal presence" means that Christ has secured having that impulse available by offering His presence at any time and forever. Here on earth, with Christian Rosenkreutz in his heart and Michael's proximity making Anthroposophy the very language of Steiner's mission, Steiner uses his life to hail and prepare

---

*   Ibid., pp. 384–385.
** Ibid., pp. 388–389.

"The knowledge of the Grail." It is "the new knowledge with the Christ mystery at its center."* Therefore, modern initiates can also be known as "Grail initiates." Grail Knowledge includes the contemplative inquiry and meditation that Steiner's verses and exercises inspire and support in those who practice them, doing so with evolving spirit awareness. By the time of the sixth post-Atlantean epoch, humanity's capacity for meditating and sharing its blessings will be much greater than it is now. Steiner's statement about Grail Knowledge means not so much that there is a window of opportunity open to us all but that the window closes at a certain time. Our meditation must begin during our *incarnated* life. After we die it is too late to begin, but if we do begin in our present incarnation we will be able to continue to avail our selves of spirit awareness when we are living outside of a physical body in the time between our death and our next life. Our present incarnation may have started already or may only soon begin, but it is highly likely that anyone reading or working with Anthroposophy in a lifetime of the fifth epoch is being initiated by her or his daily and nightly life on earth. Not necessarily as current or sometime "initiates" but as human beings of this era, our incarnation includes initiating aspects that the words of Steiner's Anthroposophy offer to open our minds and lives to our own karmas. Meditation brings consciousness to such openings.

In Steiner's *Outline of Esoteric Science*, chapter 5, "Knowledge of Higher Worlds: Initiation," specifically advises readers to look back at his great chapter 4, "The Cosmic Evolution and the Human Being," in which he clairvoyantly recorded in detail the ancient planetary evolutions of Saturn, Moon, and Earth. Why does he ask readers to look back over that vast drama of planetary evolving in chapter 4? Because the specifics with their time patterns, the roles played by the hierarchies, and the slow changes of the evolving scenes Steiner describes constitute a grand

---

*   Ibid., p. 388.

demonstration for us: When we read and reread it we recognize it to be nothing less than a record of ourselves—both of our planet Earth and of our individual relationships to it as human beings—so that we ourselves can be reminded of the spiritual scientific tasks, insight, and meditative spirituality that belongs to our ever evolving existences. Meditating as part of our existence belongs to our sacrifices and our devotion to our meditation's themes. To regard meditating in that way supports it, helps to make it worthy, and thus also combines with the spirit that the consciousness soul era places in us in our current incarnation.

There is something either superficial or ungrateful in those earthlings who fuss about whether their efforts in meditation have worth. Of course they do. Precisely because there is satisfaction to feel when we seek knowledge and notice, as we do most of the time, that we are receiving knowledge, we feel we are going in a right direction. We allow ourselves to trust our feeling about the direction we are going in and so we know that we will be experiencing subtleties with our attention. Only a misplaced attention or expectation makes it possible to let yourself complain that nothing is happening. Steiner trusts our freedom, perhaps more than we ourselves are willing to do:

> People who are still capable of becoming impatient because they "do not see anything yet" have not yet acquired the right relationship to the higher world, a relationship understood only by those who are capable of seeing the training exercises as almost an end in themselves. In actual fact, these exercises are working in our soul-spiritual nature—that is, on the astral body. Even if we cannot "see" we can feel that we are doing soul-spiritual work. The only possible reason for not being able to feel this is having a preconceived idea of what we are actually trying to "see.".... If we repeatedly say to ourselves, "I do not perceive anything," it is usually because we have preconceived ideas of how this perception is supposed to

look.... Once we have the right attitude about doing these training exercises we will increasingly find something in them that we can love for its own sake. We will wait patiently and humbly for what may follow. *

Humanity's continuing meditation will also increasingly involve the impulse of the Golgotha mystery—the birth, life, death, and resurrection of the Christ being. Our meditations help to keep the Christ's continuous benign presence in humans' soul lives and also their physical-etheric ones. Through Christianity, meditation works toward what the future brings. As the fifth Post-Atlantis epoch continues toward the sixth, meditating is creating consequence not just for our selves but for the near and farther future of humans and the planet Earth as well. Steiner advises that those human beings who are not already meditating in their current incarnations should do so, because when the sixth post-Atlantean epoch dawns, soul sensation will have become wide-spread—presumably on account of the efforts made now and for future time in the remaining fifth post-Atlantean epoch. Steiner predicts what can happen: "What we can recognize through imagination, inspiration, and intuition about the higher worlds in conjunction with the Christ Mystery will increasingly permeate our life, ideas, feeling, and will" here on Earth.**

The Hand Holding the Pen that Is Drawing the Body of the Hand Holding the Pen: The Consciousness Soul: Transforming the Astral Body to Spirit Soul and Spirit Self

During World War II, when I was in third grade in the New York City Waldorf School, I was allowed to go to a cinema theater to see my first movie, Walt Disney's *Bambi*, the story of a fawn whose loving mother dies when the forest where they live

---

*   Steiner, *Esoteric Science,* pp. 327–328 (paragraph 34).
** Ibid., p. 389.

bursts into flames leaving Bambi alone on scorched ground with the other surviving creatures. For a child who, of course, had never seen a television because it hadn't yet been invented, the impact of the film could have left me distressed. As it was the only scene of the story that I understood was Bambi snuggling with her mother early in the movie. I let the Bambi story disasters sail over my head, but the "short" that preceded the main show engraved itself on my mind and soul.

On the empty screen had appeared a hand holding a large, old-fashioned fountain pen and nib. The pen in the hand began to draw a line. As you watched the pen move over the empty screen never lifting itself off the line it was making, you began to see the line producing an arm, then a shoulder, neck, head, torso, and finally feet and legs and an arm with elbow and wrist of the very hand holding the pen. The hand holding the pen had drawn a line that comprehended the whole of the hand's own body! Instantly I could see that this surprising performance meant something, but I had no idea what. For years I occasionally returned to the puzzling riddle of what it meant to show a moving picture of a hand holding the instrument that could draw a continuous outline of the body whose hand was drawing that line.

Decades later, I met friends in their forties who were interested as I was in talking about the depths and truths of Anthroposophy's meanings for present and future times. For some reason I saw fit to mention the moving image of the pen in the hand that drew the line of the hand holding the pen. "That's the consciousness soul!" exclaimed one of the friends as soon as I had finished describing the "short." He was right. There it was; something made of nothing by something that was making the form of her or his self out of that nothing. So different from the other two "souls"—the sentient soul, receiving and responding to what comes from people and things in their environment, and the intellectual soul, at its greatest with the Scholastics of 1100 and 1200 CE, who were secluded in monasteries where they wrote elegant analyses about the existence of God or of the essences and universals in contrast to mere names, proceeding to prove their convictions with a subtlety not seen in speech and thought before or since.

Thinking critically, the thoughts of your intellectual soul tackle the nature of inner relationships with mind and perhaps heart. The consciousness soul is different. It is a soul of awareness: alert, compassionate, empathetic, open to the moment, present and capable of presen*cing* yourself. Knowing yourself to be present means that, among the other internal cognizing available to you, self-knowledge is also available to you. The consciousness soul is awake to its own self—all the more so because the "I" performs that cognizing. Whatever else Disney's modernist, self-reflexive ink drawing had been doing on the movie screen, it surely did picture the consciousness soul as Steiner describes it in both *Theosophy* (1902) and its later, deepened version, *An Outline of Esoteric Science* (1907). We know through Steiner that the consciousness soul thinking has been active in human beings since about 1500 CE, the time of Shakespeare, the time of the Renaissance, a re-birthing time. To cultivate in our souls such a potent historical period signifies a *self*-awareness that knows its selfhood to be an "I." Like the line drawn by the pen in the hand, the line that becomes visible is self-reflexive—it knows itself to be the line it draws.

The consciousness soul moves its gaze in two directions, as it were: ascending and descending. Ultimately, our double gaze identifies us with the being who came to human death in order to show us how to come to his life. We do that with our astral bodies, not with the physical, which has been created by the Divine; not with the highest beings who live within the orders of divinity; but with our human soul life which lives in between. Our consciousness soul works at the center of an evolution that depends on our actively awakened awareness of our selfhood, present—and presen*cing*—in our newly born "I." What makes the consciousness soul a different veil or garment for the soul than did the earlier ones for "intellectual" and "sentient" souls? The consciousness soul has the "I" as its task—and its capacity. As core of the human soul, it actually *adds spirit to the soul by presenting itself to* the soul, thus transforming the entire consciousness soul into *spirit-imbued* selfhood. That new selfhood characterizes our consciousness soul. The spirit self transformation has already begun. Anthroposophy calls it the Spirit Self, because it is imbued with spirit as its content. In bringing forward the Spirit Self, the astral body has transformed itself with a spirit-imbued selfhood. Much later a Life Spirit will become a transformation of etheric aspects in our physical-etheric body, and still later the Human Spirit, the Spirit *Anthropos,* will show itself as the complete, transformed human being. For now, through transformation, what used to be humanity's astral body or astral organization is becoming the spirit self in each human being. It can be called a spirit "I," higher "I," or newborn "I." It is made for meditative attention and contemplative inquiry, and it trains the humans' spirit soul.

Combining Anthroposophy and Religion: A Transformation from the Future?

"Forming Transformations from the Future" will find further considerations of the "I" as a gift of the consciousness-soul era. The considerations raise the possibility of combining Anthroposophy and religion. Anthroposophy is a spirit science not a spirit religion. It is far from wanting to become a religion in the sense of an institution that expects, even authorizes, its members to accept a religious institution's views on moral questions of their lives and interests. Steiner's Anthroposophy *does,* however, want to work with the divine, the gods of the divine, and the highly exalted divinity known as the Christ being. Since time immemorial he directed himself toward what would become the planet Earth. At the turn of time, when he was baptized after he had been on Earth for thirty years since his first birth, he lived as the true Christ being for three years of fully esoteric earthling life, who had trained to overcome death by receiving death through crucifixion and torture of his physical body on Good Friday, but remaining an esoterically divine being on earth so that he was resurrected after the crucifixion and, after forty days, ascended to heaven. Since then he lives esoterically among us, whether we are on Earth or in the heavens between our death and our return to our next earthly birth and earthly life.

Initiation in the sense of repeated earth lives has changed radically since the turn of time. Since the Golgotha mystery, if one is an initiate, one decides, with Christ of course, whether to become one in the next life. Often an initiate from one life decides to wait and go through a highly difficult lifetime in the next life so as to give of the "I" in his or her spirit self toward the needs of others. Such Christ-like offerings then become a part of the person's initiation over time, since having been an initiate at one point will be possible at another, presumably all the more so because of the sacrificial life in between.

Two anthroposophists of two different generations, both leaders of the Christian Community, which includes the church itself and the movement known as "Religious Renewal," have written about the Christ being's gift and presence in human lives since the Mystery of Golgotha.

Michael Debus is the leader of the Christian Community, as well as the seminary, both headquartered in Stuttgart, Germany. Debus's afterword to the edition of Steiner's *Christianity as Mystical Fact* wonderfully translated by Andrew Welburn takes up a highly original issue. He makes a distinction between two approaches to finding the Christ: One can *meet* him or one can *follow* him. Using these terms and instances, Debus then offers a third possibility that emphasizes both Steiner's scientific capacities and his ever-forming and deepening reverent, indeed anthroposophic, capacities. Debus's understanding of Steiner in regard to his capacities creates a way to show that Steiner does both; he encounters the Christ and follows Him, thus presenting humanity with the third possibility that Debus describes.

Emil Bock (1895–1959)—the author of the much-beloved book, *The Three Years: The Life of Christ between Baptism and Ascension*. He offers marvelous combinations of the Christ's ever-redemptive, ever-enlarging love of humanity. Bock finds these in all manner of knowledge, from the Gospels and other biblical sources, while also offering deeply imagined, inspired—even *intuited*—understanding of how the Christ met the situations during his "three years." Before coming to Debus's question, let us look at Bock's views of "die and become" and other matters. Bock's poetic and deeply meditative study of how Easter could be brought to both the simplest and most highly developed people clearly exhibits his power to tell the story. Reading Bock's almost uncanny understandings of how parallels actually describe one another—whether landscapes, history, or legends—his study becomes our knowledge.

Bock views the renewed "die and become" as pertinent to the resurrection, because the human "I" clearly engages its afterlife when shaping the next life or lives between death and the next birth. Bock takes the resurrection itself as a progressive idea. The idea of "die and become" can be found in the second panel of the Foundation Stone meditation (page 66) when the refrain of the middle verse speaks, Spirit of Light / Let there be kindled from the east / what is formed in the west / saying, *"In Christ, death become life"* (a rather wide translation of *In Christo morimur,* in Christ we die), but Steiner has made more than one translation of each of the three Rosenkreutz Latin phrases from long ago rituals in various places. Still, "in human soul making," as that Foundation Stone verse put it, the "I" can learn from the Christ being through the other mystery, that dying is the beginning (a new one each time) for transforming the karma of humans' experiences between their death and the next life. Because Christ is the "deliverer of the eternal being in the human being," his ongoing connection with dying and with returning to Earth shapes human lives through the "I" principle of each and all of us. An important key to what Bock describes in the first half of the quotation below matches the key to the lock so that there can be unity between key and door but also more moments to help and be helped as a human soul moves from death toward the next life. In the following rich paragraph Emil Bock offers a chance to take in some of the renewed meanings of "die and become":

> Since the coming into action of the new *die and become,* called by Saint Paul "to die with Christ and rise again," ... strengthening of the ego-principle in the face of destiny can now flow out from him into the lives and destinies of everyone. He quickens all that is stagnant, sets free all that is blocked. Above all, He is the Deliverer of the eternal being in the human being. In the realm of the souls who have gone through death and are preparing for a new incarnation, He loosens the knot of destiny, and in the sunlight of his being brings to blossom whatever was thwarted by the spell of material life. Through His power of overcoming death, the path of the human ego through many deaths and births becomes a *progressive resurrection* for all who unite themselves with Him.*

Bock carefully compares the old "die and become" of pre-Christian ties, with the one that now and forever holds the Good "for the inner and outer destiny of every human being" who is willing to want it. Bock says that in the temple of pre-Christian times, "die and become" signified that path taken by individually pre-ordained souls in order that, as initiates, they might attain to union with the power and wisdom of the gods. Now we are not pre-ordained by a Temple priest or chief. The "center point of time" has changed everything. Bock says:

---

*   Bock, *The Three Years,* p. 160. (my italics)

At the center point of time the Christ himself, by going through death and resurrection, placed this mystery on the open stage of ordinary human life. Since then, "die and become" has been transformed into a law which holds good for the inner and outer destiny of every human being, unless he refuses altogether to strive after higher things and gives himself over entirely to his animal nature. He who goes through "death and becoming" with the power of Christ in his heart will find in his own being that a renewal of "initiation" on Christian ground has become a reality.*

No matter where you open *The Three Years,* you feel the truth and power of the enlargement that the Christ being brought to human spiritual life on Earth and in Heaven. The enlargement is grace, not bulk, of course. The Christ shows his vital capacity for living on behalf of all those whom he carries, always easing what can be eased, always careful to keep our true being's particularity while, at the same time, making himself available to help us in danger and to offer choices that will educate us while saving us, no matter which we choose, including choosing to help others. Bock's phrase "a progressive resurrection" means that Christ's work speaks of regarding "die and become" or any aspect of death in the Bible has been extended to eternity—to *help* in eternity. Bock shows over and over how the Christ being does not rule but serves. Perhaps the most direct use of meditation happens when, after focusing, you then hold an open, empty consciousness to wait for what might come there, and perhaps then to follow it. Bock gives an extremely deep, even frightening example of Christ's own situation with his ether body in which he had dwelled for three years. It needs to be a meditation and not just a description. Bock writes:

After three days of spiritual struggle, the victory of Easter morning lay in the fact that the Christ, instead of being

---

*   Ibid., pp. 159–160.

banished by death into another world, remained on Earth in his etheric body, which had become entirely a crystal of light. At the same time, the body in which the Risen One manifests himself to his disciples was far more than an ordinary etheric body.[*]

A similarity might be what Ita Wegman, Steiner's doctor, seems to have said about Steiner's dying:

> His passing away was like a miracle. He left quite naturally. It seemed to me as if the die was cast in the last moment. And once it was cast there was no struggle, no attempt to stay on earth. For a while his gaze remained steady and calm; then he said a few kind words to me, and deliberately he closed his eyes and folded his hands. In my work as a physician I had never seen anyone pass away so quickly from the earth. The die had been cast and the other activity in the spiritual world began immediately. No further preparations were needed.[**]

In any case, it seems to me that Emil Bock's aim and technique describes lyrically and reverently (a lovely combination) the landscapes of the Christ's life in Palestine, the intricate parallels between levels of esotericism in various events, and generally a hushed yet keen atmosphere of what is described, Christ's Easter dying.

We have to meditate it to receive what he is saying, and he had to meditate it to find language with which to describe what he intuited must have been happening. Such seems to have been his way of passing to us what the gospels and other sources brought to his meditative thinking on them. Here is a continuation of

---

[*]   Bock, *Three Years*, pp. 250. It needs to be a meditation, because it is so complex, so full of goodness in every way, and so difficult to do (one can only imagine).

[**]   Selg, *Rudolf Steiner and Christian Rosenkreutz*, p. 84.

Bock's detailed description of just what had to be provided and done to make it possible for the body of Christ to arise and yet remain there with and before the disciples.*

First, Bock pauses to explain that the *quinta essentia,* the fifth essence, had "saturated...the physical body and was thus made capable of retaining form."** To explain what could be experienced next, namely that the disciples would experience something like the Christ's physical and etheric body as if they could see and feel its presence on the "plane on which they lived as creatures of flesh and blood," Bock says that "the spiritual body of the Risen One could be described either as an etheric body which had at its disposal the form and earthly faculties of an etheric physical body, or as a physical body raised out of its mortality to the plane of an etheric body." There then ensues a long list of "suprasensory experiences which tended so powerfully towards the physical plane that the disciples could believe that they perceived the Risen One with their senses. These perceptions were levels of thinking, imagination, inspiration, and perhaps intuition. The *quinta essentia,* Bock tells us, is a principle of form that holds the four elements together. I set the rest below as a quoted speech by Bock. He ends with more about the miracle of this moment with the disciples, after which he also writes a beautiful lyric about the disciples having "felt themselves transported into the scenery of a new cosmic springtime."***

> Thus the etheric body of Christ, which had been wrested from death, was in its uniqueness rightly imbued with ascent life forces and creative power. It was not a physical body, but in terms of force and form it stood in the closest possible relationship to the plane on which the disciples lived....

---

*   Bock, *Three Years,* pp. 250–251.
**   Ibid., p. 250.
*** Ibid., pp. 250–251.

In the midst of a dying earth existence, they walked in the garden of a new Earth.... In the sphere of Easter communion, the dimensions of a new cosmos open out. The miracle of bodily resurrection bridges the gulf between what is within and what is without, between microcosm and macrocosm. [Humanity's] inmost pulse of life rejoices exceedingly, [along with] the airy regions of the Earth.*

※

Michael Debus starts his discussion by showing he is fully aware that "Steiner's path to knowledge has absolutely no presuppositions. It is grounded in the experience of reality."** He knows that Steiner rejected all dogmatism of "revealed religion," in contrast to others with clairvoyance capacities who might allow themselves to indulge in trusting revelations not fully based in experienced reality. Debus notes Steiner's careful distinctions about the "I" and its life in thinking as Steiner carefully describes them in his *Intuitive Thinking as a Spiritual Path*. They show, says Debus, that "the mystery of the 'I' is...intimately connected with the essential being of thinking—the thinking that is at the same time the essential being of the world."*** Precisely this double character of the "I" interests Debus concerning Steiner's scientific basis—Anthroposophy—to perhaps serve as part of a religious understanding of life and the world, for Debus wants to show that in the matter of thinking's double connection to the "I" and to the world, Steiner's view "points to the hidden role...that Christ plays in the act of knowing."**** That "hidden role" (*not* hidden from Steiner), according to Debus, became "an entirely new element in Steiner's biography, and it opens unusual and wonderful

---

*   Bock, *Three Years*, p. 251.
**   Steiner, *Christianity as Mystical Fact*, p. 136.
*** Ibid., p. 138.
**** Ibid.

perspectives through which the Church can understand how it was born from pre-Christian mystery religions."*

Debus, who had so carefully avoided seeing Steiner's thinking as anything but scientific, now saw a shift in his understanding of Steiner as well as in Steiner's own views about the mysteries. The construction of Debus's afterword distinguishes walking a path of following Christ from a path on which one encounters him. Steiner himself came to realize a further understanding when he walked a path of *following* Christ, as distinct from one *encountering* him. For this reason, it seems that Debus decides and succeeds to show that both approaches are anthroposophic, legitimate, and useful for religious consideration.

Precisely through Steiner's writing *Christianity as Mystical Fact* (1902), especially its second edition (1910), Steiner discovered and then announced that his own work with Christianity included wanting to give more than a historical presentation of it; in addition, he says that his book *Christianity as Mystical Fact* "was meant to show how Christianity came into being, *from the standpoint of a mystical awareness.*"** Continuing his description of working with this view of Christianity, Steiner quickly shows that his viewpoint is actually scientific as well as mystical, though he knows all too well that few scientists, who only include matter and not spirit, can accept that combination:

> I have based my work...on the idea that the achievements of modern science lead over into a genuine mystical view-point. To deny such a possibility, from this point of view [i.e., not accepting the mystical one], is actually a con-tradiction of the scientific attitude that underlies those achievements. The epistemological conclusions, claimed by so many to be the only ones grounded in the facts of

---

*   Ibid., pp. 141–142.

**   Ibid., p. 126 (emphasis added).

science, are in reality quite unable to explain the scope of that natural science itself. *

Meanwhile, Debus, whose argument has been absolutely clear that Steiner first encountered the Christ being by means of his usual path of "no presuppositions,"—the path "grounded in the experience of reality that is possible for every human being" as Debus puts it—can now also show that a churchly need is not necessarily for *encountering* Christ but can be equally important for *following* him. Debus finds that Steiner himself realized at a certain point that "The Mystery of Golgotha" could also be regarded in a non-scientific way, the way of perceiving and honoring that "the creative power at work in Christianity was actually *preparing the ground for its own appearance* in the pre-Christian Mystery-cults."** Ultimately Debus saw that Steiner's scientific basis for teaching himself the truths of the Christ's divine and earthly existence did not cancel the value of regarding seriously the religious powers alive in the Mystery of Golgotha, even though Steiner himself did not need or choose to use them.

Debus wants to make it possible that Anthroposophy can take a religious position toward the Christ. His wise and brilliant essay favors perceiving Steiner as one who has *followed* Christ, despite and in addition having first found Christ through the scientific certainty that was based on no presuppositions. Debus's understanding of Steiner's twofold intimacy with Christ, which Steiner himself had undoubtedly experienced, gently distinguished *following* Christ from *encountering* Him. Either approach, or even both of them, could apply to any human being's finding the Christ. Debus clearly describes and certifies the churchly path that he himself had sought by closing his argument as follows so that Steiner's participation in it is clear and honored:

---

*   Ibid.

**   Ibid., p. 127.

Anyone who seeks knowledge by beginning the path without presuppositions of any worldview whatsoever will
sometime at some point on the path, no matter how far-
distant, eventually meet Christ.

The direction is reversed in the spiritual stream of the
Church, which is not the principle of *encounter* but the
principle of *following*. This path is therefore not without presuppositions; it is based instead on a pre-existing
relationship to, and experience of, Christ himself, who
becomes the leader of whoever follows him. Steiner
speaks of this for the first time in *Christianity as Mystical
Fact*. It was not possible in 1902 to present everything in
a fully developed form. The second edition in 1910 is a
further development and clarification, and also, in part, a
supplement to what was said in 1902.*

At this point, Debus points to the following from the second
edition of Steiner's *Christianity as Mystical Fact*:

I have based my work ... on the idea that the achievements
of modern science lead over into a genuine mystical
viewpoint. To deny such a possibility, from this point of
view, is actually a contradiction of the scientific attitude
that underlies those achievements.... In the pages that
follow, I emphasize that Christianity presupposes earlier
mysticism as a seed presupposes a place to grow. The
study of Christian origins will serve to bring out, rather
than to obscure, the unique nature of Christianity.**

Debus continues:

Apparently, after the turn of the century, Rudolf
Steiner found himself in an entirely new situation.
He had devoted himself with complete selflessness to
the methods of thought of other people. This became

---

*   Ibid., p. 142.
**   Ibid., pp. 126–127.

for him a path of thought leading to knowledge of Christ, indeed to Christ himself. Solemnly standing before the Mystery of Golgotha as foundation, Steiner could now immerse himself also in the ecclesiastical stream, with understanding. This is an entirely new element in his biography and it opens unusual and wonderful perspectives through which the Church can understand how it was born from pre-Christian Mystery religions. Such an understanding is new and unprecedented in the history of Christianity....

On this path forged by Steiner the experience of Christ shows us that the essential being of the world *comes to meet* our human thinking. Anyone who seeks knowledge by beginning the path without the presupposition of any worldview whatsoever will sometime at some point on the path, no matter how far-distant, eventually meet Christ.

The direction is reversed in the spiritual stream of the Church, which is not the principle of *encounter* but the principle of *following.**

Debus's complex, creative, and courageous approach to his theme seems a worthy form of the "I"-consciousness. That is why the afterword of our handbook includes it. Debus's intricate thought, so carefully presented, honors Steiner's Anthroposophy while also trying to open Steiner to the idea that *following* the Christ is as equally legitimate a form of reverence as is the scientific way of no pre-perceptions.

Debus's church-based appreciation of Steiner's Anthroposophy being able to find Christ in both ways—encountering and following—has much depth in its own right. Like many others, I admire both its writing and its thinking. Second, meditating to experience suprasensory existences can happen more fluently the more the meditating soul has awareness, which is the

---

*   Ibid., pp. 141–142.

consciousness soul's main gift to the spirit soul. As meditator, you undertake to become one with the theme by focusing on *its* existence, rather than on yours. Being a spirit self as part of the consciousness soul culture liberates your attention to the gesture of researching. Choose a theme, if you wish to meditate that theme's existence. For instance, what inner help or lessons or other gifts can come from *following* Christ, and how such gifts might come only to someone who begins with no pre-perceptions but waits to become informed.

Finally, Debus's clarity about how Steiner proceeded and spoke about his relationship to the Christ being is actually an argument about the "I." Anthroposophy shows that what is known as "the higher "I" is, in fact, the very being who holds all of us within himself, every single "I" without exception. To me, that "answer" is rich in feeling meditations—gratitude, interest in specifics, examples of the goodness that the higher "I" realizes that Christ's accompaniment to you or his gifts to your particular situation make you come to realize this meditatively and then hold it gently in your heart by means of your will.

On the last page of the afterword in *Christianity as Mystical Fact,* Debus has a final paragraph that tells us the paths are merging. Steiner started an approach of merging for the first time. His experience at the turn of the century (with follow-ups later that, I think, are all in German) gave Steiner substances of Christianity, independent of any documents. Because it is that kind of substance, I suppose it is still different from other straight knowledge that Steiner previously had only the encountering kind of path. So it's partly encountering and partly merging.

> Thus, a union of the two paths is created, which can be called *Anthroposophy*. For this reason, depending on the direction from which one approaches it, Anthroposophy is either the working of knowledge without any presup- positions or comprehensive knowledge of Christ. In

Christianity as Mystical Fact, Rudolf Steiner bore witness
to the latter approach for the first time. This book contains anthroposophic Christology in germinal yet comprehensive form.*

It is a delight to read this argument, which is so clear and
so carefully constructed that you find you have actually heard it
twice and, on the second time, heard it as a solution.

❋

Christ is the highest form of the "I." Each human being has and
develops a version of the Christ, the highly exalted one who lives
for the life of humanity and has done so since he first started
preparing to come to Earth as the Word made flesh and the one
who died there on the cross in order to be resurrected *and* dwell
with humanity on Earth and in Heaven for all time thereafter.
The Christ is the highest "I," and he is a human "I" because
he exchanged his godhood for human selfhood everlastingly. In
short, for meditating, nothing is more fitting than to know, as
best you can at any particular moment, that the "I" you have
in your very constitution is part of the "I" that Christ also has,
and yet is nevertheless your own. Initiate or murderer—or both—
each and every human being at any height or lowness can come
toward Christ's high and gracious presence as he comes toward
us. He and we live *in* one another.

In the following quotation from a lecture by Steiner,
"Perceiving the Christ through Anthroposophy," his words and
thoughts offer what meditating individuals who turn to the
Mystery of Golgotha and to Anthroposophy can find—"true religious feeling and knowledge of our own suprasensory nature."
Here is the heart of Steiner's wish for those who turn toward
their suprasensory capacities with their modern hearts—that is,
those who with their souls teach themselves how to meditate,
alone and with others:

---

*   Ibid., p. 147.

Although exoteric science has made us free and achieved great outer triumphs, it has also instilled very understandable doubts in our hearts with regard to religious feeling and knowledge of our own supersensible nature. Anthroposophy, which works out of the spirit of science, has taken up the task of eliminating these doubts and implanting truly religious life in the human soul. Far from contributing to the death of religion, Anthroposophy will foster a revival of religious feeling and a new understanding of Christianity, which can be correctly understood and accepted only by turning to the Mystery of Golgotha.

Because anthroposophically derived spiritual knowledge will not only revive old religious feelings but also enkindle new ones, it is safe to say that *Anthroposophy harbors no sectarian aspirations. This is as true of anthroposophy as it is of any other science.*[*]

With these assurances, we who want to meditate can include ourselves in Steiner's aspirations and, in turning our souls to the Golgotha mysteries, can also turn to meditation. May this handbook support those efforts.

❈

---

[*]   Steiner, *The Sun Mystery and the Mystery of Death and Resurrection*, p. 124 (emphasis added).

To the Gods

W. S. Merwin

When did you stop
telling us what
    we could believe

when did you take
    that one step
only one
above
all that

as once you stepped
out of each of the stories
about you one after
    the other
and out of whatever
we imagined we
    knew of you

who were the light
to begin with
and all of the darkness
at the same time
and the voice in them
calling crying
and the enormous answer
neither coming nor going
but too fast to hear

you let us believe
the names for you
whenever we heard them
you let us believe
    the stories
how death came to be
how the light happened
how the beginning began
you let us believe
all that

then you let us believe
that we had invented you
and that we no longer
believed in you
and that you were
    only stories
that we did not believe

you with no
moment for beginning
no place to end
one step above
all that

listen to us
wait
believe in us

W. S. Merwin's poem, "To the Gods," is addressed to the gods but clearly speaks of humanity's relationships to them. It ends with three short lines that seem to add a new thought: *"listen to us / wait / believe"* You could hear those lines as a prayer, as an urgent cry, as a new possibility, or all three.

Cited and Relevant Works

Works by Steiner

Anthroposophical Leading Thoughts: Anthroposophy as a Path of Knowledge: The Michael Mystery. London: Rudolf Steiner Press, 1998.

Autobiography: Chapters in the Course of My Life, 1861–1907. Great Barrington, MA: SteinerBooks, 2006.

Christianity as Mystical Fact: And the Mysteries of Antiquity (tr. and foreword by Andrew Welburn; afterword by Michael Debus). Great Barrington, MA: SteinerBooks, 2006.

Curative Education cited; current edition, *Education for Special Needs: The Curative Education Course*. London: Rudolf Steiner Press, 1998.

Esoteric Lessons 1904–1909: From the Esoteric School, vol. 1. Great Barrington, MA: SteinerBooks, 2007.

Esoteric Lessons 1910–1912: From the Esoteric School, vol. 2. Great Barrington, MA: SteinerBooks, 2013.

Esoteric Lessons 1913–1923: From the Esoteric School, vol. 3. Great Barrington, MA: SteinerBooks, 2011.

Eurythmy as Visible Speech. London: Rudolf Steiner Press, 1984.

The Foundation Stone Meditation: Three English translations with the original German. London: Rudolf Steiner Press, 2005.

Four Mystery Dramas: The Portal of Initiation, The Soul's Probation, The Guardian of the Threshold, The Souls' Awakening. Great Barrington, MA: SteinerBooks, 2007.

From the History and Contents of the First Section of the Esoteric School 1904–1914: Letters, Documents, and Lectures. Great Barrington, MA: SteinerBooks, 2010.

How to Know Higher Worlds: A Modern Path of Initiation. Hudson, NY: Anthroposophic Press, 1994.

Intuitive Thinking as a Spiritual Path: A Philosophy of Freedom. Hudson, NY: Anthroposophic Press, 1995.

An Outline of Esoteric Science. Hudson, NY: Anthroposophic Press, 1997.

The Redemption of Thinking: A Study in the Philosophy of Thomas Aquinas. Spring Valley, NY: Anthroposophic Press, 1983.

The Riddles of Philosophy: Presented in an Outline of Its History. Great Barrington, MA: SteinerBooks, 2009.

Speech and Drama. Great Barrington, MA: SteinerBooks, 2007.

Start Now! A Book of Soul and Spiritual Exercises. Great Barrington, MA: SteinerBooks, 2004.

The Sun Mystery and the Mystery of Death and Resurrection: Exoteric and Esoteric Christianity. Great Barrington, MA: SteinerBooks, 2006.

Theosophy: An Introduction to the Spiritual Processes in Human Life and in the Cosmos. Hudson, NY: Anthroposophic Press, 1994.

A Way of Self-Knowledge: And the Threshold of the Spiritual World. Great Barrington, MA: SteinerBooks, 2006.

Works by Other Authors

Bock, Emil. *The Three Years: The Life of Christ between Baptism and Ascension.* Edinburgh: Floris Books, 2006.

Dickinson, Emily. *The Complete Poems of Emily Dickinson.* New York: Little, Brown, 1960.

Harwood, A. C. *The Recovery of Man in Childhood: A Study in the Educational Work of Rudolf Steiner.* Great Barrington, MA: The Myrin Institute, 1958.

Kühlewind, Georg. *Becoming Aware of the Logos: The Way of St. John the Evangelist.* Hudson, NY: Lindisfarne Press, 1985.

———. *From Normal to Healthy: Paths to the Liberation of Consciousness.* Hudson, NY: Lindisfarne Books, 1988.

———. *The Gentle Will: Guidelines for Creative Consciousness.* Great Barrington, MA: Lindisfarne Books, 2011.

———. *The Light of the "I": Guidelines for Meditation.* Great Barrington, MA: Lindisfarne Books, 2007.

———. *Stages of Consciousness: Meditations on the Boundaries of the Soul.* Hudson, NY: Lindisfarne Press, 1984.

———. *Working with Anthroposophy: The Practice of Thinking.* Hudson, NY: Anthroposophic Press, 1992.

Lipson, Michael. *Group Meditation.* Great Barrington, MA: SteinerBooks, 2011.

———. *Stairway of Surprise: Six Steps to a Creative Life.* Great Barrington, MA: SteinerBooks, 2002.

Lowndes, Florin. *Enlivening the Chakra of the Heart: The Fundamental Spiritual Exercises of Rudolf Steiner.* London: Sophia Books, 2005.

Prokofieff, Sergei O. *May Human Beings Hear It! The Mystery of the Christmas Conference.* London: Temple Lodge, 2004.

Prokofieff, Sergei O., and Peter Selg. *The Creative Power of Anthroposophical Christology: An Outline of Occult Science, The First Goetheanum, The Fifth Gospel, The Christmas Conference.* Great Barrington, MA: SteinerBooks, 2012.

———. *The Foundation Stone Meditation: A Key to the Christian Mysteries.* London: Temple Lodge, 2007.

Selg, Peter. *Rudolf Steiner and Christian Rosenkreutz.* Great Barrington, MA: SteinerBooks, 2012.

———. *Rudolf Steiner and the School for Spiritual Science: The Foundation of the "First Class."* Great Barrington, MA: SteinerBooks, 2012.

———. *Rudolf Steiner as a Spiritual Teacher: From Recollections of Those Who Knew Him.* Great Barrington, MA: SteinerBooks, 2010.

———. *Rudolf Steiner's Foundation Stone Meditation: And the Destruction of the Twentieth Century.* London: Temple Lodge, 2013.

Whitman, Walt. *Leaves of Grass.* New York: Viking, 1961.

Zajonc, Arthur. *Meditation as Contemplative Inquiry: When Knowing Becomes Love.* Great Barrington, MA: Lindisfarne Books, 2008.

Zeylmans van Emmichoven, F. W. *The Foundation Stone.* London: Temple Lodge, 2002.